Landmarks of world literature

Stendhal

THE RED AND THE BLACK

Landmarks of world literature

General Editor: J. P. Stern

Dickens: *Bleak House* – Graham Storey
Homer: *The Iliad* – Michael Silk
Dante: *The Divine Comedy* – Robin Kirkpatrick
Rousseau: *Confessions* – Peter France
Goethe: *Faust. Part One* – Nicholas Boyle
Woolf: *The Waves* – Eric Warner
Goethe: *The Sorrows of Young Werther* – Martin Swale
Constant: *Adolphe* – Dennis Wood
Balzac: *Old Goriot* – David Bellos
Mann: *Buddenbrooks* – Hugh Ridley
Homer: *The Odyssey* – Jasper Griffin
Tolstoy: *Anna Karenina* – Anthony Thorlby
Conrad: *Nostromo* – Ian Watt
Camus: *The Stranger* – Patrick McCarthy
Murasaki Shikibu: *The Tale of Genji* – Richard Bowring
Sterne: *Tristram Shandy* – Wolfgang Iser
Shakespeare: *Hamlet* – Paul A. Cantor
Stendhal: *The Red and the Black* – Stirling Haig
Brontë: *Wuthering Heights* – U. C. Knoepflmacher
Pasternak: *Doctor Zhivago* – Angela Livingstone
Proust: *Swann's Way* – Sheila Stern

STENDHAL

The Red and the Black

STIRLING HAIG

Professor of French, University of North Carolina at Chapel Hill

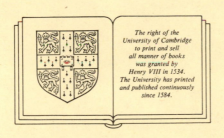

The right of the
University of Cambridge
to print and sell
all manner of books
was granted by
Henry VIII in 1534.
The University has printed
and published continuously
since 1584.

CAMBRIDGE UNIVERSITY PRESS

Cambridge
New York   New Rochelle   Melbourne   Sydney

Published by the Press Syndicate of the University of Cambridge
The Pitt Building, Trumpington Street, Cambridge CB2 1RP
32 East 57th Street, New York, NY 10022, USA
10 Stamford Road, Oakleigh, Melbourne 3166, Australia

First published 1989

Printed in Great Britain at
the University Press, Cambridge

British Library cataloguing in publication data
Haig, Stirling
Stendhal: The red and the black.—
(Landmarks of world literature).
1. Fiction in French. Stendhal, 1783–1842.
Rouge et le noir
I. Title   II. Series
843'.7

Library of Congress cataloging in publication data
Haig, Stirling.
Stendhal: the red and the black / Stirling Haig.
        p.   cm. – (Landmarks of world literature)
ISBN 0–521–34189–2. ISBN 0–521–34982–6 (pbk.)
1. Stendhal, 1783–1842. Rouge et le noir.   I. Title.
II. Series.
PQ2435.R72H35   1989
843'.7 – dc19   88–39787   CIP

ISBN 0 521 34189 2 hard covers
ISBN 0 521 34982 6 paperback

GG

Contents

Acknowledgements

For moral and material support indispensable to the writing of this book, I wish to thank the Camargo Foundation and its Director, Michael Pretina, Terence Moore of Cambridge University Press, the University of North Carolina at Chapel Hill, Professor Victor Del Litto, Professor Lorin Uffenbeck, Professor J. P. Stern, and my wife, Judy.

Note on translations

Translations from *Le Rouge et le Noir* are my own. I have quoted from the authoritative edition established by Henri Martineau, first for the Divan edition of Stendhal's complete works (*Le Rouge et le Noir*, 2 vols., Paris, 1927), then for the Pléiade edition (*Romans et nouvelles*, vol. 1, Paris, 1952). References in the English translations are to part and chapter number.

Chronology

	Stendhal's life and writings	Major literary events	Important historical events
1782		Laclos, *Dangerous Liaisons*.	
1783	23 January Henry Beyle born in Grenoble.		
1784		Beaumarchais, *The Marriage of Figaro*.	
1785		Chénier, *Idylls*.	
1787		Schiller, *Don Carlos*. Bernardin de Saint-Pierre, *Paul and Virginia*.	Ratification of the US Constitution.
1789			French Revolution.
1790	Death of his mother.	Blake, *The Marriage of Heaven and Hell*.	
1791			Approval of the US Bill of Rights.
1793	His father listed as 'notorious suspect'.		Execution of Louis XVI and Marie-Antoinette; dechristianisation campaign.
1793–4	Visits the Society of Jacobins.		
1794			Celebration of the Supreme Being; fall of Robespierre.
1795			The Directoire.
1796–7			French victories in Italy.
1796–9	Attends the new Ecole Centrale at Grenoble.		

1797–9			
1798		Hölderlin, *Hyperion*. Foscolo, *Last Letters of Jacopo Ortis*. Coleridge and Wordsworth, *Lyrical Ballads*.	Nelson destroys French fleet at Aboukir Bay.
1799	Arrives in Paris, fails to enrol in *Ecole Polytechnique*.		Bonaparte's *coup d'état* of 18 Brumaire.
1800	Enters government service, arrives in Italy; discovers the opera and Milanese society.	Novalis, *Sacred Songs*. Mme de Staël, *On Literature*.	Establishment of prefectoral system; independence of Haiti.
1801		Chateaubriand, *Atala*. Schiller, *Maria Stuart*.	
1802		Chateaubriand, *The Genius of Christianity*.	The Concordat reintroduces Catholic practice in France.
1802–4	Returns to Paris; resigns commission; studies theatre and acting; discovery of philosophy of 'Ideologue' Destutt de Tracy.		
1803			Louisiana Purchase.
1804			Promulgation of Civil Code; coronation of Napoleon as Emperor.
1805	Lives in Marseille with actress Mélanie Guilbert.	Chateaubriand, *René*. Schiller, *Wilhelm Tell*.	Battles of Trafalgar and Austerlitz.
1806–11	Serves in war commissaries in France, Prussia, Austria, and Hungary.		

Year			
1808			Establishment of the University.
1810			Napoleon divorces Joséphine, marries Marie-Louise of Austria.
1811	Leave of absence; returns to Milan to 'conquer' Angela Pietragrua.	Goethe, *Faust*, Part I. Kleist, *Michael Kohlhaas*, *The Prince of Homburg*. Mme de Staël, *On Germany*. Austen, *Sense and Sensibility*.	
1812	Leaves for Russia; sees burning of Moscow and Grande Armée's retreat. *(1812–13)*		Russian campaign begins; occupation of Moscow.
1813	Obtains sick leave; arrives in Milan.	Byron, *Childe Harold's Pilgrimage*. Austen, *Pride and Prejudice*. *(1812–18)*	
1814	Helps organise defence of Dauphiné; returns to Milan and travels in Italy; his largely plagiarised first book appears: *The Lives of Haydn, Mozart, and Metastasio*.	Scott, *Waverley*. Byron, *Lara*.	Allies invade France; Napoleon abdicates; return of Louis XVIII; Congress of Vienna.
1815	Lives in Milan. *(1814–21)*		Napoleon's return from Elba; battle of Waterloo (18 June).
1816	Meets Byron.	Austen, *Emma*. Hoffmann, *The Devil's Elixirs*. Constant, *Adolphe*.	
1817	*The History of Painting in Italy* and *Rome, Naples, and Florence* (first work to be signed 'Stendhal').	Hoffmann, *Night-Pieces in Callot's Manner*. Byron, *Manfred*.	

1818	Meets his great unrequited love, Métilde Dembowski.	Allied occupation of France ends.
1818–21		First steamship crossing of
1819		Atlantic.
	Austen, *Persuasion*.	
	Byron, *Don Juan*.	
	Austen, *Mansfield Park*.	
	Keats, 'To a Nightingale', 'On a	
	Grecian Urn', 'On Melancholy'.	
	Scott, *Ivanhoe*.	
	Shelley, 'Ode to the West Wind'.	
	Schopenhauer, *The World as Will*	
	and Representation, vol. 1.	
	Leopardi, *Canzoni*.	
1819–22		Carbonari uprisings in Italy;
1820	Composes his epitaph: *Visse*,	accession of George IV.
	scrisse, amò ('He lived, he wrote,	
	he loved').	
	Lamartine, *Poetic Meditations*.	
1821	Suspected of revolutionary	Death of Napoleon.
	sympathies, he is obliged to leave	
	Milan; arrives in Paris; in London	
	sees Kean perform *Othello*.	
1821–9		War of Greek independence.
1822	Frequents Parisian salons and	Independence of Brazil.
	writes for French and English	
	periodicals; *De l'Amour*.	
	Byron, *Cain*.	
1823		Monroe Doctrine.
1823–4	*Racine and Shakespeare; The Life*	
	of Rossini; returns to Italy	
	(Florence and Rome).	
1824		Succession of Charles X.

1824–5	Return to Paris and freelance journalism; *Racine and Shakespeare II*; death of Métilde Dembowski.		Decembrist uprisings in Russia; first railway line (Stockton and Darlington).
1825		Pushkin, *Boris Godunov*.	
1826	End of his stormy affair with Clémentine Curial; travels to London and north of England.	Chateaubriand, *The Natchez*. Cooper, *The Last of the Mohicans*. Heine, *Book of Songs*. Vigny, *Cinq-Mars*.	
1827	*Armance*; travels in Italy (Naples, Rome, Florence, Milan).	Hugo, Preface to *Cromwell*. Manzoni, *The Betrothed*. Poe, *Tamerlane*.	
1828	He is expelled from Milan by the Austrian police.		
1829	*Promenades in Rome*; affair with Alberthe de Rubempré.	Balzac, *The Last Chouan*. Irving, *Chronicle of the Conquest of Granada*. Mérimée, *Chronicle of the Reign of Charles IX*. Musset, *Tales of Spain and Italy*.	
1830	Giulia Rinieri declares her love; *The Red and the Black*; named consul in Trieste.	Hugo, *Hernani*. Lamartine, *Poetic and Religious Harmonies*.	July Revolution; advent of Louis-Philippe; capture of Algiers; independence of Belgium.
1830–42		Comte, *Positive Philosophy Course*.	

1831	Refused by the Austrians, he is appointed consul in Civitavecchia (Rome's seaport).	Hugo, *Notre-Dame de Paris*. Dumas, *Antony*. Balzac, *The Wild Ass's Skin*.	Reform Bill.
1832	Often absent from his post, travels widely in Italy; writes *Memoirs of Egotism*.	Roethe, *Faust*, Part II. Sand, *Indiana*. Vigny, *Stello*. Pellico, *My Prisons*.	
1833	Discovers the manuscripts that will become the *Italian Chronicles* (one will develop into *The Charterhouse of Parma*); meets Alfred de Musset and George Sand on their way to Italy.	Balzac, *Eugénie Grandet*. Michelet, *History of France*, vols. 1 and 1. Pushkin, *Eugen Onegin*. Sand, *Lélia*.	
1834	Begins *Lucien Leuwen* (unfinished).	Musset, *Lorenzaccio*.	Revolt in Lyon; rue Transnonain massacre.
1835	Begins *The Life of Henry Brulard* (unfinished).	Balzac, *Father Goriot*. Tocqueville, *On Democracy in America*, Part I. Vigny, *Chatterton*; *Military Servitude and Grandeur*.	
1836	Begins an extended, three-year leave in Paris.	Musset, *The Confession of a Child of the Century*.	Attempted coup of Louis Bonaparte.
1836–7			
1837		Dickens, *Pickwick Papers*. Carlyle, *The French Revolution*. Hawthorne, *Twice-Told Tales*. Sand, *Mauprat*.	Accession of Victoria.

1837–8	Publishes several stories of the *Italian Chronicles*; travels in France, Switzerland, Holland, Belgium that yield the *Memoirs of a Tourist*.		
1837–9		Dickens, *Oliver Twist*.	
1837–43		Balzac, *Lost Illusions*.	
1838		Hugo, *Ruy Blas*.	
1838–9		Dickens, *Nicholas Nickleby*.	
1839	Publication of *The Charterhouse of Parma*; begins his last novel, *Lamiel* (unfinished).		Chartist riots; photography invented.
1839–40		Lermontov, *A Hero of Our Times*.	
1840	Return to Civitavecchia; reads Balzac's article on *The Charterhouse* and begins revisions (abandoned); writes 'The Privileges of 10 April 1840'.	Hugo, *Sunbeams and Shadows*. Mérimée, *Colomba*. Poe, *Tales of the Grotesque and Arabesque*. Scribe, *The Glass of Water*.	Translation of Napoleon's ashes to Invalides; second attempted coup of Louis Bonaparte.
1840–1		Dickens, *The Old Curiosity Shop*. Tocqueville, *On Democracy in America*, Part II.	
1841	First apoplectic attack; obtains sick leave, returns to Paris.	Cooper, *The Deerslayer*. Emerson, *Essays, First Series*.	Anglo-French entente.
1842	23 March Dies of a stroke on a Paris street.	Balzac, Foreword to the *Human Comedy*. Gogol, *Dead Souls*.	

Chapter 1

The Red and the Black: the background

Perduto è tutto il tempo
Che in amar non si spende

Stendhal's worlds

Henri Beyle, whom the world knows under the most celebrated of his multiple pseudonyms, Stendhal, is the author of a landmark of European literary realism, *The Red and the Black*. Yet even had Stendhal not published this novel, today seen as a monument in a mode or school he himself never heard of (for, if 'realism' is a coinage of the 1820s, it only gained currency well after his death), he could claim our attention as the author of one of the world's most subtle and unusual treatises on love, *De l'Amour*. Moreover, he is the author of an autobiography that can fairly be said to rival Augustine's or Rousseau's *Confessions* for its candour and its consciousness of the problems the genre poses the writer who would be simultaneously subject, object, and writing agent. This is *The Life of Henry Brulard*. Finally, Stendhal would certainly be remembered for his second great novel, *The Charterhouse of Parma*. And this is to leave unmentioned other novels, finished and unfinished, his travel writings (he is said to have virtually invented the concept of modern tourism), biographies of composers and studies of painters, journals, reflections, and polemical writings such as his *Racine and Shakespeare*, an important document in the history not of realism, but of romanticism.

The wide range of his writings, moreover, points to something else that the chronology of the previous pages will confirm: Stendhal came late to his career as a novelist (his first novel, *Armance*, was not published until 1827), and he was fully 47 years of age at the publication of *The Red and the Black.* Henri Beyle was quite aware of the instability of his own temperament − a modern trait, this seems to us with our suspicion regarding any assertion or assumption of a unitary self − and certainly projected it onto Julien Sorel, whose chief characteristic (a redeeming one, it should be noted at the outset) is his *imprévu*, or unpredictability. It is this concern for earnest self-scrutiny that is the impetus, only five years after *The Red and the Black*, for the undertaking of *The Life of Henry Brulard* which, along with his *Journal* and *Souvenirs d'égotisme*, provides the chief source of our knowledge of his life. Since Stendhal (totally unlike Flaubert, for example) is an author in whom there is a constant and intense interpenetration of the personal and the fictional, *Henry Brulard* is a text that warrants space in our discussion, both for its relevance to *The Red and the Black* and for its inherent interest. Many of its themes − the Oedipal conflict and the search for career and love − are transposed into *The Red and the Black* in such a way that fiction, for Stendhal, becomes a personal essay and quest for inner truths, as well as an aesthetic undertaking.

'Henry Brulard' is Henri Beyle's *alter ego* of the same initials, a distancing construct that Beyle instituted in order to recapture with integrity a past that was avowedly only accessible by means of imaginative reconstruction. 'What eye can see itself?' is the crucial acknowledgement in chapter 1. To this extent, *Henry Brulard* is like a novel − the novel of Stendhal's youth. We shall find the very same passion for veracity and truth-telling in *The Red and the Black*, whose epigraph is 'The truth, however harsh'. Yet Stendhal also had a passion for secrecy (codes, signals, and secret hiding places play a large role in *The Red and the Black*) and provided at least four different title pages describing *Henry Brulard* as a novel imitated from Goldsmith. This is the most waggish of them: 'To the Police. This is a novel imitated from *The Vicar of Wakefield*. The hero, Henry Brulard, writes his life at age 52, after the death of his wife, the famous Charlotte Corday [Marat's assassin]. Beginning of the work, volume 1. I, Henry Brulard, wrote what follows in Mero [Rome] from

1832 to 1836.' And Stendhal did indeed begin writing the work at age 52 — but that was in 1835, not the date of 1832 given in the text, a date no doubt chosen because of its climacteric significance: the fateful age of 50, the time most men set to sum up their accomplishments and existence. *Henry Brulard* begins with its narrator standing on the Janiculum hill in Rome on a virtually cloudless, sunny October day. Let us call him HB, to indicate the overlap between the historical personage and the fictional persona, between Henri Beyle and Henry Brulard. In both fiction and autobiography, truth was the thing:

I'm writing this without lying, I hope, without fooling myself, with pleasure like a letter to a friend. What will that friend's ideas be like in 1880? How different from our own! . . . This is new for me: to speak to people about whom one knows nothing — their way of thinking, their type of education, prejudices, religion! What an encouragement to be *truthful*, and simply *truthful*: that's the only thing that counts . . . How many precautions must one not take in order not to lie!

HB assures his future reader that he can only vouchsafe the feelings of his past. He readily concedes that his memory may be faulty, and repeatedly compares his past to a fresco with missing pieces; and throughout his autobiography HB is careful to make sketches of floor plans, street layouts, rough maps of Grenoble and the countryside in a documentary effort to pin down the veracity of his memories.

HB readily acknowledges that he was a rebellious youth; in fact he detested his father. Like Julien Sorel, he felt and indeed willed himself an outsider. For all his life he would remain something of a *frondeur* and a perpetual lover, hating monarchy and the Church as institutions, but loving aristocratic tastes and manners, and creating sympathetic portraits of fictional priests, like Chélan and Pirard, revering the idea of democracy and the pursuit of happiness, but disdaining the mercantile conformity and cultural mediocrity of the United States (his model of a modern republic) and shunning contact with the 'people'. HB's rebellion against authority was of a nature both political and paternal —

mostly the latter. Indeed, *Henry Brulard* sets forth the classic elements of the Family Romance:

> I wanted to cover my mother with kisses and there not to be any clothes. She loved me passionately and embraced me often; I returned her kisses with such ardour that she was often obliged to leave. I abhorred my father when he would interrupt our kisses. I always wanted to give them to her on the breast. It should be remembered that I lost my mother in childbirth when I was barely seven years old.

HB tries to explain for his 1880 reader what the Grenoblois character is like by reference to Père Sorel in *The Red and the Black*; but he then muses that by 1880 his novel will probably have crossed over the 'dark edge' of oblivion. He realised that literary fame — of which Stendhal enjoyed rather little in his lifetime — was a chancy matter. Thus he joked he had taken a ticket in a lottery whose grand prize was this: to be read in 1935.

The mother — by contrast with his father, Chérubin Beyle, whom he represents as money-grubbing, petty-minded, and repressive — fit into a growing personal mythology of the artistic, sensitive maternal soul alert to the finer sentiments of life. In *The Red and the Black* in particular, there is a fictional projection of young HB's situation: first, of the fused maternal and the erotic in Julien's love affair with the older Mme de Rênal; and second, of the paternal conflict with the repulsive figure of Père Sorel, and the thematic quest for a suitable father figure that begins with abbé Chélan and continues through the Marquis de la Mole. With *Tom Jones*, which he much admired, HB had once shared what might be termed the foundling fantasy: 'Might I not be the son of a great prince?' *The Red and the Black* will thematise this personal question, integrating it into the perennial conflict of generations, and raising it to the level of an implicit inquiry into the legitimacy of authority conferred by origins.

A crucial fact of Stendhal's intellectual and sentimental life is that he was born in 1783, six years before the Revolution. Thus, unlike Balzac and Victor Hugo (his *literary* contemporaries), who were born respectively in 1799 and 1802, and who were very much men of their time — thoroughly Romantic — Stendhal straddles the eighteenth and nineteenth centuries, the Enlightenment and Romanticism.

In this respect the three authors' attitudes toward the greatest personality of the age is revealing. Balzac and Hugo fixed upon the grandiose and legendary aspects of Napoleon; indeed, Hugo's naïve but successful mythologising of the Napoleonic saga played a definite role in preparing the advent of Napoleon III — and thus his own exile. And Balzac, whose novels are for the most part set in the Restoration, aspired during his entire career to the composition of a grandiose war novel — whence his admiration for the Waterloo episode of *The Charterhouse of Parma*. But Stendhal, the Imperial administrator, while harbouring his own ambiguous admiration for the heir to the liberal values of the Revolution, had also observed the tyrannical aspects of the Napoleonic regime. He had seen at first hand the burning of Moscow, witnessed the disastrous retreat of the Grande Armée, observed the horrors of war from close range. He had a soberer, or sobered, view of the Emperor. Julien Sorel's greatest shortcoming is to view life through a Napoleonic prism.

Thus Stendhal's complex temperament was formed by two very different historical and cultural periods. It combines a logical and analytical approach to life and letters with an enthusiastic abandon (*espagnolisme*) that is unique. Stendhal can be both the man of ironical detachment and of unrestrained exuberance; both remote and involved, rational and passionate. His books benefit immensely from this combination of spontaneous narrative flow and tongue-in-cheek interventions. (Stendhal's irony will be discussed in chapter 2.)

When very young HB decided to write comedies, with Molière as his model. (This ambition was to endure for years and years before he turned at last to the novel.) He did not advance very far, believing that it was necessary to await inspiration — 'the moment of genius' — in order to write. 'If I had mentioned my writing project, some sensible man would have told me: "Write for two hours a day, genius or no." This advice would have saved ten years of my life foolishly spent in waiting for *genius*.' But HB could not be a writer of comedies (which is not to say that he could not be a comic writer) because of his *espagnolisme*. This admiration for the ideal, the lofty and generous sentiment, made him recoil before vulgarity and mediocrity. Molière's Chrysale (in *Les Femmes savantes*) with his measured, bourgeois good sense, he found depressing: 'The conversation of a true bourgeois on *men and life*, which is only a collection of these ugly details, throws me into deep *spleen* [melancholy] when propriety obliges me to listen to him for some time.' Stendhal will project this boredom into his rendition of M. de Rênal's conversation and Mme de La Mole's salon. But this 'horror of Chrysale', this inability to focus on a hard-headed, commonsensical approach to life, had advantages. Stendhal never lost his capacity for enthusiasm, never became morally blasé. This spirit of youth – even of youthful folly, of *espagnolisme* – informs all his works, and particularly the character of Julien Sorel.

HB's first formal educational experience came with the Republic's decision to create a system of *Ecoles centrales*. The chief architects of these lay schools were Joseph Lakanal (for whom a famous Parisian lycée is named) and Antoine Destutt de Tracy, coiner of the term 'ideology' (which for him meant the study of ideas and how they are acquired). As a philosopher, Tracy emphasised the logical and conscious aspects of the mind; Stendhal later came to know him and to revere him as an intellectual mentor. He may even have had something to do with Stendhal turning to fiction, for Tracy once told him that 'Nowadays one can only get at the truth through the novel.' The *Ecoles centrales* stressed science and mathematics, as well as European (i.e. not exclusively French) *belles-lettres*; and drawing, history of art, modern languages, and history were also included. (The *Ecoles* were eventually abolished by Napoleon.)

His favourite subject soon became mathematics. He was strongly attracted by a discipline that depended on logic, for he was passionately committed to reason and truth.

Mathematics did not admit of hypocrisy; and, he began to realise, it was a means of escaping Grenoble to further his education in the capital. 'Supreme happiness was to live in Paris writing books on an income of 100 louis.' Success in mathematics eventually did give him a chance for the *Ecole polytechnique*, the prestigious school of engineering in Paris. It was, at last, his ticket out of Grenoble. As his father was waiting to put him on the coach, HB noticed that he was softly crying. What HB next wrote he admits was not nice: 'The only impression his tears made on me was to find him quite ugly.'

The discovery of Italy; early writings

HB was but 16 when he left Grenoble. He arrived in Paris on 10 November 1799, the day after Bonaparte's *coup d'état* of 18 Brumaire, a neat coincidence that marked the beginning of a new life for HB, and a new epoch for France and Europe. Paris was at first a disappointment: he was repelled by the food, the muddy streets, and the absence of mountains. He seems to have had no intention of sitting for the *Ecole polytechnique* entrance examination, nor to have entertained other notions of what to do with himself at all. Soon he fell quite ill, and was rescued from a quack doctor and insalubrious quarters by the intervention of some distant cousins, the powerful Daru family. They moved him into their fine *hôtel*, or private mansion, for his convalescence. HB would have liked to devote himself to an artistic career, but the practical Darus soon found him employment as a lowly clerk in the war ministry. Like Julien, HB experienced excruciating boredom at having to dine with his patrons and put in appearances at their salon. And, like Julien, he committed the small but revealing error of misspelling a common word, *cela*, with two l's, *cella*: 'So this was the man of letters, this the brilliant humanist who disputed the merits of Racine and who had carried off all the prizes in Grenoble!'

Work at the ministry was heavy, for the First Consul was secretly reorganising the army for a campaign in northern

Italy. It would cross the Great St Bernard Pass and strike against the Austrians. In May 1800, HB was summoned to join the Darus in Milan. He was deliriously happy at this prospect of adventure. His route took him through Geneva and other places rich in memories of Rousseau and *La Nouvelle Héloïse*, which he read as he rode, learning some hard lessons in horsemanship along the way. (Julien, along with other Stendhalian heroes, undergoes a virtual rite of equestrian humiliation.) HB was wild with joy upon arriving in Italy; now he had seen where happiness lay: 'To live in Italy and hear such music became the basis for all my reasonings.' All his life he was passionately fond of vocal music: 'I would go ten leagues on foot through the mire, the thing I detest most in the world, to attend a well-played performance of *Don Giovanni*. If one Italian word of *Don Giovanni* is pronounced, at once the tender memory of the music comes back to me and takes its hold.'

For Stendhal, as for so many European travellers, such as Goethe and later Browning, Italy was a revelation. Yet Stendhal was no doubt marked more deeply than any of them by the discovery of a land that became his anti-France, as it were, and he contributed (and succumbed) perhaps more completely than any other literary figure to the Romantic myth of Italy. Not only was Milan one of Europe's intellectual capitals in the eighteenth and early nineteenth centuries, but to Stendhal Italians were more passionate and much more forthcoming than the French. They were spontaneous and authentic, 'natural' in a word, and utterly unconcerned with the personal vanity and fear of what others might think that made the French so watchful – and thus hypocritical. Stendhal admired their fiery energy, a Renaissance-like *virtù*, which persisted in France, he thought, only among the lower classes, where strong emotions were still to be found. Crimes of passion thus attracted him; they play a large role in the plots of his *Italian Chronicles* and in the revenge of La Sanseverina in *The Charterhouse of Parma*. It was this manifestation of emotional energy that aroused his interest in the Berthet and Lafargue affairs (see pp. 15–17) and formed the broad outlines of the story line of *The Red and the Black*. Although he return-ed to France after eighteen months, and was not to see it again for ten years, Italy remained his chosen heartland.

From 1802 to 1806, Stendhal lived mainly in Paris, where he furthered his personal studies through intensive reading; Stendhal must have recognised that he was not after all a man of action, and as a sincere republican he experienced growing disenchantement with Napoleon's increasingly authoritarian ways. A military career would have been as unsuitable for him as for Julien Sorel, for the very idea of regimentation was alien to their natures. Stendhal's studies at this time centred on the eighteenth-century sensationalists (Locke, Condillac, Helvetius) and their disciples, the *Idéologues*, whose chief representatives were Cabanis and Tracy. All notions derive from the senses − that is the proposition that sums up their thought. Stendhal's desire to understand human nature, com-bined with his love for the theatre (early aroused in Greno-ble), led him to seek a 'science of the heart' in the comedies of Molière. He began work on two verse plays. The mastery of psychological principles would rationally lead him to literary composition. An ambitious list of 1803 sets forth plans for the writing of four comedies, seven or eight tragedies (including a *Hamlet* and an *Othello*), two epic poems (a *Paradise Lost* and an *Art of Love*), and three histories, the latter to be begun at age 35. As a complete *homme de théâtre*, he decided to learn acting, and ended up following an actress to Marseille.

From 1806 to 1814, Stendhal enjoyed success as a middle-level Imperial administrator, and even as a salon dandy. In 1811 he spent the autumn months travelling to Milan, Florence, Rome, and Naples, and formed the first ideas for a book on Italian painting. In 1812 Napoleon embarked on his ill-starred Russian campaign, and Stendhal followed him there, arriving in time to witness the burning of Moscow, the horrors of the winter retreat, and the beginning of the end of the Imperial regime. In 1814 he resigned his position and took up residence in Milan for the next seven years, a period during which he acquired a thorough knowledge of Italy. In 1815, his love for music yielded his first publication, *The Lives of Haydn, Mozart, and Metastasio*. This work was almost entirely plagiarised, a fact Stendhal scholars dismiss as the peccadillo of an apprentice learning his trade. His second book was *The History of Painting in Italy* (basically limited to the Florentines), and in the same year came *Rome, Naples, and Florence in 1817*. With this book he settled upon the pseudonym by which we know him today. ('Stendhal' is supposedly taken from the name of a small German town.) Stendhal had seemingly launched a career as an expatriate biographer, critic, and travel writer. Indeed, at the end of 1817 he had started on a biography of Napoleon. It was early in 1818 that he met the great love of his life, Mathilde Viscontini Dembowski (he always called her Métilde). The living and the writing of this love lasted through June 1821, and became *De l'Amour*.

The structure of the book is very loose, consisting of short chapters ranging in length from a few lines to a few pages, written in the deliberately 'dry', pithy style that Stendhal so admired in Montesquieu. Despite the title, *De l'Amour* could scarcely be compared to a modern sex manual or even a 'pop' psychological study of male – female relations. It is by turns analytic, anecdotal, and historical; and it is mainly personal therapy. Among its famous features are the five, later seven stages of love's evolution from surprise and admiration to desire, hope, and 'crystallisation'. By this famous term Stendhal meant the transformation that the loved one undergoes in the eyes of the lover. All the loved one's traits undergo a brilliant heightening or transformation – a process affirmed in Proust's dictum that to see a woman and to see a woman one loves are two completely different matters. *De l'Amour* also catalogues four types of love: (1) passionate love, in the manner of Abelard and Héloïse; (2) *amour-goût*, a love based on shared predilections in culture and background, and whose examples he found in eighteenth-century Parisian society; (3) purely physical attraction; and (4) vanity love, an artificial kind of love based on status or riches. The last chapter contains a famous comparison between Don Juan and Werther, Goethe's tender and tragic hero. While Don Juan's physical satisfactions are many, and Werther's few or none, the latter must nevertheless be considered happier because of the triumphs of his imagination: he enjoys 'realities fashioned according to his desire'. One of the book's most startling insights is this: the greatest happiness in love comes from 'the first squeeze of the hand of a woman we love'.

De l'Amour is often viewed as a source book for the treatment of love in *The Red and the Black*. It is indeed tempting to align the stages of love and the development of Julien and Mme de Rênal's love, or to detect in Julien and Mathilde de La Mole what Stendhal writes about jealousy, or again to find in Mathilde the embodiment of vanity love (or *amour de tête*). Mathilde's name obviously invites comparison with Métilde's, and although most critics would locate her closest fictional incarnation in the Mme de Chasteller of *Lucien Leuwen*, Stendhal did compare Métilde to an 'Herodiade' by the Renaissance painter Luini, or to Salome − a link with Mathilde's bearing off the severed head of Julien in the closing scene of *The Red and the Black*.

By this time Stendhal was engaged in the Romantic battle. If the new school were to triumph over the old, it would have to do so on the stage, for it was in the theatre that French Classicism had achieved its greatest triumphs. Thus, much of the debate between defenders of Classicism and adherents of Romanticism revolved about questions of dramatic practice. Stendhal's fame in Parisian literary circles dates from his publication of *Racine and Shakespeare* (1823, with an enlarged version in 1825).

Stendhal argues from a position of cultural and historical relativism. The theatrical reforms he seeks are rather limited: a theatre written in prose, treating national subjects, and renouncing the unities. Shakespeare was thus the grand exemplar for the renewal of French theatrical practice. Apropos of comedy, Stendhal later wrote this in the margins of his own copy of *The Red and the Black*: 'Ever since democracy filled the theatres with gross people incapable of understanding refined things, I consider that the novel is the Comedy of the nineteenth century'; there, too, he quoted Tracy to the effect that truth today can 'only be reached in the novel'.

Armance, Stendhal's first novel, appeared at last in 1827. Today, *Armance* may seem a tedious book, unreadable to all but Stendhal's most fervent devotees. The subject of the novel — the hero's secret impotence — had been suggested by two recent literary treatments of the scabrous theme, and Stendhal himself had written of 'fiascoes' in *De l'Amour*. But the secret of Octave de Malivert is so understated and handled with such discretion (literary decorum required it) that contemporary readers, deprived of all but the most indirect allusions to Octave's dilemma, were unable to penetrate the mystery. The novel failed. At the suggestion of his cousin Romain Colomb (later to be his literary executor), he set himself to composing a new travel book, *Promenades in Rome*.

The *Promenades* contain remarks on the fine arts (Michelangelo, Bernini, etc.), and are also a guide to the Colosseum, St Peter's, the Capitol, the Raphael rooms in the Vatican, and so on — what one might expect to find today in a Michelin 'Rome in Ten Days' sort of itinerary. The book's principal interest lies in its Stendhalian tone: remarks on the Italian character, anecdotes concerning convent intrigues, details of assassinations — manifestations of that *énergie* he so admired. After the narrating of these adventures, some of which stretch out to short-story length, it is almost with regret that he returns to the business of writing a guide book. Here is evidence of the novelist in Stendhal coming irresistibly to the fore. In the *Promenades* we find Stendhal's observation on Napoleon that so clearly applies to Julien:

Because an artillery lieutenant became Emperor, and raised to the heights of society two or three hundred Frenchmen born to live on an income of a thousand francs, a mad and necessarily unhappy passion has gripped all the French . . . In the presence of the greatest gifts, a fatal blindfold covers our eyes, we refuse to recognise them for what they are, and forget to enjoy them.

Along with Italian stories about the disorders of the Papacy and tales of conspiracy, Stendhal also recounts the Lafargue trial — a French affair — which clearly constitutes our bridge to *The Red and the Black*.

Lafargue was a sinister young cabinet maker who fired two pistol shots at his unfaithful mistress and then slit her throat. Lafargue was found guilty, but sentenced to a short term despite his horrible crime (probably because of the girl's tarnished reputation). Stendhal thought the case demonstrated how passionate feelings had deserted the French upper classes to take root in the petty bourgeoisie, 'young men who, like M. Lafargue, have received a good education, but whose absence of means forces them to work and sets them struggling with true needs'. He draws a parallel with Napoleon, who combined the same circumstances: 'good education, ardent imagination, and extreme poverty'. The elements common to Julien and Lafargue are their strong effect on the trial jury; their haughtiness and pridefulness; the pistols rented from a gun dealer who also loads their weapons; their interest in 'philosophical ideas'; and their character: Stendhal writes of Lafargue that he has 'an energetic and fastidious character'. The idea of *The Red and the Black* is in gestation in these pages.

Soon after the appearance of the *Promenades*, Stendhal left Paris for a trip to the south of France and Spain. He returned by way of Marseille, and it was there, during the night of 25–26 October 1829, that 'the idea of Julien' (as he referred to *The Red and the Black*) came to him. He started to work immediately, and returned to Paris about a month later with a first draft of the novel. Stendhal was about to embark on the greatest period of his creative life; the landmark publication of *The Red and the Black* in 1830 was followed by the redactions of the unfinished *Life of Henry Brulard* and *Lucien Leuwen*. (*Lucien Leuwen* is as much the mirror of the July Monarchy as *The Red and the Black* is of the Restoration.) The publication of *The Charterhouse of Parma* came in 1839, and was hailed by Balzac as a masterpiece. In fact, Balzac's magnificent tribute is perhaps the most glowing ever paid by a great novelist to his peer during the lifetime of both.

Chapter 2

The Red and the Black: the novel

Sources

We have seen that by 1830 Stendhal was already the author of a considerable body of published and unpublished works. Although he was now a skilled writer, his reputation, for the reader of the times, would have been quite modest, at best that of a journalist or polemicist. As a novelist, a few knew of him as the anonymous author of the undistinguished *Armance*. Yet *Armance* set the tone for Stendhal's greater novelistic achievements in at least three ways: it is derivative (the plot was adopted from Mme de Duras's novel, *Olivier*), it is grounded in contemporary history (the salons of 1827), and the main character's conduct seems enigmatic and even unintelligible. It already introduces its reader to the problematic reciprocities of the real and the imaginary, the self and the world, 'Mr Myself' and 'Stendhal'.

Since Stendhal's name is forever linked with the aesthetics of the mirror (to avoid the vexed term of 'realism' for the moment), it is worth noting that the preface to *Armance* introduces this specular metaphor, which returns time and again in relation to Stendhal's novels. The authors of a recent comedy 'presented a mirror to the public; is it their fault if some ugly people passed in front of the mirror? What side is a mirror on?' The mirror of art — it is an ancient image that we can trace back to *The Republic* (Book X), where Plato says that everything can be produced 'provided that, a mirror in your hand, you consent to walk it in every direction'. In *Armance*, Stendhal seems to be exempting the art of the mirror from the rigors of moral and political criticism: it is a neutral reflector (he argues) that cannot modify or veil what

14

it encounters. In fact, the problem of *Armance* is precisely a matter of self-censorship, for Octave's inexplicable behaviour toward his beloved is determined by his secret impotence. The secret was not revealed in the novel, as we have seen, but rather in a private letter to Prosper Mérimée. This may serve as a double warning of sorts. First, Stendhalian narrators play an ironical, teasing game of hide-and-seek (French says it better: *cache-cache*) with their readers; their affirmations must always be considered suspect, or at least playful, at a first level. Second, every novel of Stendhal's has 'supplements'. *The Red and the Black* gains from a reading of two of his short stories (*Vanina Vanini* and *Mina de Wanghel*), and should certainly be read with particular reference to Stendhal's own book review (printed as an appendix in the best French editions of the novel), a 'puff-article' intended for an Italian journal. The review raises a number of points regarding realism in *The Red and the Black*. We shall encounter the mirror again in our path, but for now, let us look briefly at the novel's composition.

While many of Stendhal's themes, notably the lack of energy in nineteenth-century France, are adumbrated in earlier works, it is commonly recognised that Stendhal's creative imagination could only function once it was grounded in a firm plot outline − always a borrowed one, for Stendhal was not a gifted inventor. In a marginal note to *Lucien Leuwen* he wrote that he could not carry off a witty dialogue and think of the background at the same time: 'Whence the advantage of working with an already given story, like Julien Sorel.' (This is also the case for *The Charterhouse of Parma*.) The anchoring texts − the catalysts for *The Red and the Black* − were the accounts of murder trials that Stendhal read in the *Gazette des Tribunaux*, a newspaper specialising in sensational court proceedings. Stendhal's fancy was taken by two stories recounted there, the Lafargue case related in *Promenades in Rome*, and the Berthet case. The latter was even closer to Stendhal, for the trial took place in his home department of the Dauphiné. Berthet was an aspiring theology student who became tutor to the children of M. and Mme Michoud. Berthet claimed that Mme Michoud seduced him, that he was eventually forced out of the Michoud household, and supplanted in his mistress's affections by another young tutor. Failing to complete his seminary studies, Berthet obtained another tutor's post, this time with the Count de Condon's family, and was again expelled after accusations of an affair with the Count's daughter. Blaming the Michouds for his misfortunes, Berthet began sending a series of threatening letters to Mme Michoud, and told several people that he intended to kill her. Entering church one Sunday morning during mass, he fired a double-shotted pistol at Mme Michoud, grievously wounding her. He turned a second pistol on himself, but succeeded only in breaking his jaw. Berthet was convicted of premeditated, voluntary homicide and sentenced to death.

In addition to the points of convergence listed above, the newspaper account of the trial and Stendhal's novel share a number of features. The courtrooms are both packed with elegant ladies; as the trial begins, the accused man's pallor, his physical slightness and reputed intellectual gifts attract attention (as they had earlier, when the village priest gave him the rudiments of his education). Both protagonists are denounced by jealous servants, and retire to isolated places in natural surroundings to meditate. Berthet, like Julien, admitted premeditation, and again, Julien-like, he hotly denied that he once failed to appear for a duel: the place had not been agreed on, 'otherwise I wouldn't have missed the meeting'. Both are sensible of the social vulnerability attending an aristocratic young lady's interest in them, a lady who by virtue of her birth and wealth could aspire to a brilliant match.

In the eyes of the public prosecutor and the court reporter, Berthet's crime was motivated by disappointed ambition, wounded self-esteem, jealousy, and a desire for vengeance: the belief that the lady 'was not at all a stranger to his humiliations and to the obstacles that closed off the career he had dared aspire to'. Here we can recognise Julien's impulsive reaction to Mme de Rênal's letter to the Marquis de la Mole, as we can his state of mind as Berthet travels to the scene of the crime: 'I was so beside myself that I could barely recognise a path I had often taken; I was almost unable to cross a bridge on the path, so troubled was my vision! . . . my thoughts were churning and incoherent; I didn't know where I was; the past and the present seemed to merge; my very existence seemed a dream to me . . .' Berthet may have been attempting with these words to establish a defence of temporary insanity, but it would be hard to deny, except for the motive of jealousy, that Stendhal's narration follows this source quite closely. This is an important issue, for Stendhal's detractors allege that Julien's attempted murder of Mme de Rênal is out of character for the calculating ruser who has taken Tartuffe as his model; champions of his psychological insight cite as the motivating factor Julien's fiery independence, which in the end they relate to his disinterestedness and nobility of soul. Julien's crime will come up for discussion later. The point for now is to underscore Stendhal's intense involvement in his own age, his 'modernity' (in *Racine and Shakespeare*, we have seen, he defended Romanticism and its contemporaneity against French Classicism, suited for our 'great-grandfathers'), and to point to the role that history plays in *The Red and the Black*, whose subtitle terms it a 'Chronicle of 1830', and whose first epigraph calls for 'The truth, however harsh'.

The mirrored age

The first observation to be made on 1830 as the date in the subtitle of *The Red and the Black* is the absence from the novel of that year's signal event in France, the July Revolution. It put an end to the Bourbon monarchy, and issued in the reign of a constitutional monarchy that was to last until another upheaval with deeper social consequences was to wrack France, the Revolution of 1848. An introductory note assures the reader that the novel was written in 1827; but events referred to in the text are indeed from 1830 (for example, an allusion to the première of Hugo's *Hernani*, which marked the victory of the Romantic revolution in literature), and it has been demonstrated that the internal chronology of the novel runs well into 1831. When Stendhal actually began his novel is in dispute, despite his precise notation – 1828 or 1829? In his projected book review, Stendhal constantly referred to his portrait of *1829* society. It seems clear that he was outchronicled, as it were, by history – overtaken once his novel was nearly finished by the great event that he could not conveniently incorporate into his text. Thus the virtual ellipsis of 1830's main event in this 'Chronicle of 1830'. (In a 1928 film version of *The Red and the Black* by Gennaro Righelli, Julien dies on the barricades!) Stendhal's novel is more a period portrait – Restoration France – than the record of any single year.

There were actually two restorations of the Bouron monarchy. The first, in 1814, after the crumbling of the Empire, was interrupted by Napoleon's return from exile in Elba – the Hundred Days – and the second, which came after his defeat at Waterloo in 1815. The second Restoration brought a military occupation of France and exacerbated the class tensions and hostilities that were the legacy of the Revolution. From the Revolution in 1789 to Napoleon's final departure in 1815, political and social change – and war – had radically transformed France. Many aristocrats who fled the excesses of the Terror had lived difficult, sometimes meagre, existences in foreign lands. They had seen their ancient rights and privileges revoked; and along with their allies, the clergy, their land holdings and estates had been confiscated in the name of the Nation as *biens nationaux* (national property). Few of them were chastened by their exile, and many expected to be restored to their former situation or to be compensated for their losses. The Law of Indemnification was an attempt to address their grievances. The returning exiles were faced with a new class of landowners who had no intention of disgorging their newfound source of sustenance and independence. The exiles were regarded with hostility by those who deemed they had returned 'in the baggage train of the foreigner', and they were denounced for 'having learned nothing – and forgotten nothing'.

Louis XVIII attempted to exercise his power in moderation, and to follow policies of conciliation. A Charter (not a constitution) was 'granted' to his people; it confirmed new property owners in their legal rights, asserted the principle of equality for all before the law, and established legislative chambers. These policies won him the support of republicans and Bonapartists (who were lumped together as the 'liberals'), as well as the bourgeoisie, which hoped for peace and economic stability, and the Church, which hoped to reestablish the traditional power alliance between altar and throne. They earned the king the opposition of the intransigent royalists known as the 'ultras'. This faction is portrayed in the 'Secret Note' episode of *The Red and in Black* (II, 21), where the reactionary plotters hope to achieve a new military occupation of France by foreign monarchies in order to purge France of 'liberal' elements and tendencies. The ultras thus rage against the liberals and the 'usurper' *Buonaparté*. (The Italian pronunciation and spelling serve a double purpose: they emphasise his un-Frenchness and are intended as an ethnic slur.) The ultras' head was the Count d'Artois (the King's brother), *plus royaliste que le roi*. Fewer than 100,000 persons qualified for the vote (and fewer than 15,000 were actually eligible), so the regime was scarcely a representative one. The ultras' power was greatly increased by public revulsion at the assassination of the Duke de Berry, the only nephew of the childless king who could have children. In the aftermath of the Duke's death, control over the university was tightened, individual freedoms were restricted, and press censorship was reinstituted. Liberals were forced underground and into unsuccessful political actions.

The Count d'Artois succeeded his brother to the throne in 1824 as Charles X. The new king was theocratic by temperament, and thus open to clerical influence. One of the earliest laws of his reign concerned sacrilegious acts, which became punishable by death when committed in a church. Religious missions and manifestations, such as the Bray-le-Haut ceremonies evoke (I, 18), became widespread and generated anticlerical opposition in the bourgeoisie, which purchased new editions of Voltaire and *Tartuffe* (Molière's play about religious hypocrisy and power-seeking that Julien has memorised). Books thus represent subversive liberalism, and Julien, because of his delicate position as an aspirant priest, dares not set foot in the Verrières bookstore. The historical Bishop of Périgueux was actually on record as stating that 'two arsenals of vice and corruption' plague every French city: the brothel and the bookstore (*cabinet de lecture*).

The French Church traditionally enjoyed what were termed 'the Gallican liberties', that is, a practical measure of administrative independence from Rome in non-doctrinal matters. This is why advancement for Julien would come more readily from M. de La Mole or Mme de Fervaques than from the Church hierarchy. But the French Church was torn by strife (exaggerated by Stendhal for dramatic purposes) between worldly, supple Jesuits (abbé Castanède's name sounds vaguely Hispano-Inquisitorial) and austere, unworldly Jansenists. (The latter were strict and unaccommodating, and were sworn enemies of the Jesuits.) Thus abbé Pirard, the Jansenist, is a dangerous protector for Julien to choose, even though he is the titular director of the seminary.

The pervasive influence of the secretive Congrégation – of which Stendhal makes a great deal in *The Red and the Black* – was widely feared. Abbés Castanède and Frilair are Stendhal's figures of this sinister organisation devoted to restoring the pre-eminence of the faith and the clergy in post-Revolutionary France. We see their influence in Verrières (I, 23), where they arrange for one of their faithful to obtain a cheap lease on a piece of valuable town property, thus angering the local businessmen. Those who contribute generously to the Congrégation's charities, like Valenod, are rewarded, whereas M. de Rênal, who makes the mistake of giving too little, is frowned upon. 'The clergy doesn't take such matters lightly', observes the narrator. Indeed, in a rather comic reversal that occurs after Julien has moved to Paris, Valenod (now the Baron *de* Valenod) becomes mayor when it is learned that M. de Rênal is really a 'liberal'.

Because French liberals were acquiring electoral ambitions,

the provinces were turning into a political battlefield. The blame for these social tensions is attributed to Napoleon in the beginning of Part II of *The Red and the Black*. As Julien travels by coach to his new career in Paris, he listens to a conversation in which a 'philosopher', Saint-Giraud, denounces his friend Falcoz's Bonapartism: Bonaparte reintroduced the vogue for nobility (with his *noblesse d'Empire*) into a France that had been largely 'cured' of it; Bonaparte, with his Concordat, returned the priests to positions of influence instead of treating them like ordinary citizens. (Observing their power in Verrières, the fourteen-year-old Julien stops speaking of Napoleon, and 'announced his intention of becoming a priest'.) Needless to say, Julien's admiration for the Emperor is unaffected by this criticism; his first action upon arriving in the capital is to pay a visit to Malmaison, Josephine and Napoleon's château.

In 1829, a centrist government yielded to the ultra Polignac ministry, which further disturbed a bourgeoisie now moving into France's belated industrial revolution. M. de Rênal is a figure caught in the social and political flux of these contradictory tendencies. He is a royalist (as mayor, he has constructed a *Cours de la fidélité)*, but he is also a factory owner. We see him annoyed at the increasing wealth of Verrières's *industriels*, people who have 'no origins' and who may even be 'Jacobins' (i.e. 'Reds'). His faith in conservative politics extends to his three sons, who are respectively destined, in the manner of the *ancien régime*, for the army, the law, and the Church.

New elections in 1830 produced a majority for the opposition. When Charles X sought to dissolve the new Chamber, to restrict freedom of the press – in sum, virtually to abrogate the Charter – Paris rose in armed insurrection. After three revolutionary days known as the *Trois Glorieuses* of 27–29 July, Charles X was on his way to exile in England. Although a republic might have been the logical successor to monarchy, with La Fayette at its head, in 1839 the word 'republic' still evoked memories of the guillotine. Conservative political manoeuvring ensured the advent of a 'bourgeois monarchy' headed by the Duke d'Orléans, who reigned as Louis-Philippe.

Facts and fiction

This is the socially and politically unstable France that serves as background to *The Red and the Black*. Stendhal incorporated history into his novel on at least three levels, and these contribute to its 'realistic' armature. First, Stendhal cites a number of purely autobiographical items: Julien's admiration for the cavalry was Stendhal's own; the double 'l' misspelling of *cela* was his, as we have seen; Prince Korasoff's system is described in his correspondence. MM. Appert and Gros were real-life people. At this level of history with a small 'h', Stendhal also introduced into his novel some of the petty dealings that transpired in Verrières, and no doubt in less fictional villages: the profitable realignment of a stream, rake-offs on purchasing, road-building, and the undervalued leasing of communal property. Of the same cloth in a loftier social class are the Marquis de La Mole's profitable buying and selling of government bonds based on what today's stock markets know as 'insider trading'. To a friend, Stendhal wrote in 1834: 'In describing a man, a woman, or a place, always think of someone or something real.'

Stendhal's taste for realistic detail was based on his respect for the 'small true fact' acquired from the *Idéologues*, for whom truth derives from experience, and he regularly made use of what he called *pilotis* – things or events based on reality that could be embroidered by the author's imagination. At this level, however, one can note that lengthy descriptions are not to his taste. He condemned them in Sir Walter Scott, and once wrote that the boredom of composing them long kept him from writing novels. If Stendhal perhaps sacrifices to convention in the opening description of Verrières – but much of the description is symbolic, like the retaining walls of the Rênal property – we may take his presentation of Julien's first days in Paris as more typical. The narrator provides no information about where Julien lodges upon his arrival, and barely mentions the mansard of the Hôtel de La Mole that Julien occupies a few days later. As for the great townhouse itself, we learn only that it was constructed during a period devoid of architectural distinction (II, 1) and that Julien's admiration for it is thus a mark of his provincialism. The overall impression made by the rooms is 'as sad as it is magnificent'; the narrator is sure that his readers would refuse to inhabit them. There are no descriptions of the dresses worn by Mme de Rênal or Mathilde de La Mole, and in his book review Stendhal specifically scorns such concern for petty detail.

In addition to this aversion to description, Stendhal prefers to present many actions from the perspective of the character, rather than from that of the all-knowing narrator. This foreclosure of understanding — the ellipsis of experience — produces a freshness of presentation ('defamiliarisation') that often bears comic overtones. Two examples are Julien's encounter with Amanda Binet in the Besançon café (I, 24), and his fitting for new clothes in Paris (II, 2).

When Amanda bids Julien sit near her, she shows him just where by leaning over the counter, 'which gave her', the narrator adds with Voltairean understatement, 'an opportunity to show off a superb figure. Julien observed this; all his ideas were changed.' Soon Julien is telling Amanda that he loves her 'violently', and is reciting from his prodigious memory passages from *La Nouvelle Héloïse*. He will recite the same text in Mathilde de La Mole's bedroom and be tendered in return a studied compliment in which Mathilde is chiefly attentive to manipulating an unfamiliar grammatical person, the *tu* of intimacy. Similarly, when abbé Pirard leads Julien into a series of great rooms in Paris, Julien is totally puzzled as he is greeted there by an elegant man with a pleasant manner: 'Julien made a half-bow. The gentleman smiled and placed a hand on his shoulder. Julien started and leapt backwards. He turned red with anger. Abbé Pirard, despite his seriousness, laughed till the tears came. The gentleman was a tailor.' The immediacy of perception, but also the discontinuity and staccato rhythms contribute to the comedy of these pages. Julien can make no intellectual connections between gesture and intention. The actions thus remain uncoded for him, that is, they lie outside the reassuring ambit of social intelligibility.

On a second level of borrowings from life, Stendhal accomplishes integration of mimesis and semiosis: that which is imitated from life is so woven into the fiction as to play a simultaneous structural or thematic role. The Bray-le-Haut episode ('A King in Verrières', I, 18) has been linked to various religious manifestations organised by the Congréga-tion to restimulate faith among the masses, such as would lead to the erection of an enormous cross near Rouen in 1821. Claude Liprandi has shown that it is also based on the transla-tion of the relics of St Vincent de Paul from Notre Dame to a Lazarist chapel at the beginning of 1830. Stendhal read a newspaper account of the ceremony in *Le Moniteur* of 1 May 1830. An entire sentence passed almost word-for-word from the newspaper into the novel's description of the church: 'Since the numerous windows of the church were covered in crimson material, a stunning light effect resulted in the sun's rays, of the most imposing and religious sort.' The wording in the novel (I, 5) is only slightly modified, and the borrowing neatly demonstrates the point concerning Stendhal's realism: as will be the case for Balzac, and later for Flaubert and Zola, the semiotic process lies in the transformation of the 'small true fact' into a point of literary significance. Partaking of both, the fictional church description is at once a 'mirror copy' of external reality and coded to the semantic system whose core concept is death.

Thus 'crimson' resembles 'blood', and this is offered as the 'logical' explanation for Julien's impression that there is blood on the floor: 'Upon leaving, Julien thought he saw blood near the fount. It was some spilled holy water; the reflection of the red curtains covering the windows made it look like blood.' The proleptic death watch of the novel is blazoned by sanguinary allusions initiated in the title and its epigraph (attributed to the guillotined Danton), and con-tinues through the portrayal of St Clement, Altamira at the ball in Paris (there is a price on his head), Mathilde's cult of her beheaded ancestor, Mme de Rênal's shooting, to Julien's own end. In the citation above, the cliché phrase 'to spill blood' is quasi-actualised, and there are even stronger intimations of death in the scrap of newspaper Julien reads concerning the execution, in Besançon, of one Louis Jenrel. 'Who can have put this paper here?' wonders Julien in a moment where the text foregrounds the artifice of its own operations. (Who indeed, if not the Author?) Then he sighs, 'Poor wretch, his name ends like mine', not seeing that Louis Jenrel is an exact anagram of his own name. The church visit portends Julien's own end.

Finally, we cannot refrain from connecting 'crimson' and 'blood' with the red of the novel's title. At this third level, we reach the supra-historical or symbolic realm of Stendhal's signifying practices. With *The Red and the Black*, Stendhal struck upon one of the most arresting fictional titles in world literature. According to Romain Colomb, the title came to him all at once; previously he had merely referred to the work as 'Julien', and toyed with 'Seduction and Repentance' as a title. There has been much discussion over the years about the title's precise meaning, and it is clearly the critics' desire for preciseness, with its limiting effect, that has raised objections to nearly every interpretation so far put forward. The earliest readings attribute *red* to Julien's desire to rise through a military career. The byword of the Napoleonic era was 'careers open to talent' − as opposed to the *ancien régime*'s reliance on birth alone for making one's way in the world − and in another evocation of social mobility that would have appealed to Julien's ambition, all of Napoleon's soldiers were said to be 'carrying a marshal's baton in their knapsacks'. *Black*, posing fewer problems of interpretation, would be related to the colour of the cassock, 'the colour of my century', thus to Julien's decision to seek advancement in the Church. Indeed, Julien's double vocation seems to come out in the 'King in Verrières' episode, where he rushes from the honour guard to his place in the religious procession, leaving, much to abbé Chélan's annoyance, his spurs sticking out from beneath his cassock. Red and black could also be political colours: Revolution and Reaction.

Objectors point out that there is no obvious link between red and Napoleon's army (the 'redcoats' were after all notoriously British), and that *blue* is the colour of the Restoration army Julien so happily joins as a cavalry lieutenant. Other interpretations deduce the title from gambling, relating red and black to the colours on a roulette table (there are problems of French gender with this, however), the two aspects of Julien's love affairs, and the range of ecclesiastical ambitions available to Julien (from the humble black of the private secretary/priest to the red of the cardinalate).

If the ultimate aim of the historical 'chronicle' novel is to sum up an age − the fulfilment of literary mimesis (the representation of the real) − it must achieve this at a general conceptual level that raises the reader above a potentially random accumulation of details and scenes. At this third level of signification, the title serves another type of descriptive function. While making a somewhat different point, F. W. J. Hemmings once glossed the title of *The Red and the Black* for us in a way that is broad, yet sufficiently nuanced to retain focus: 'for a post-Napoleonic generation, the road to fortune is coloured black, and not red (being the winding path of intrigue, hypocrisy, petty infamies, instead of the earlier royal road of virile, full-blooded valour)' (*Stendhal. A study of his novels*, p. 115). Red and black are then the reversing poles of the novel's tensions, the generators of its incessant thrusting movement.

Questions formal and structural

Epigraphs

Turning the pages of *The Red and the Black*, the reader cannot avoid being struck by the proliferation of chapter titles, epigraphs, and running heads that Stendhal has placed on nearly every page of his text. It is not entirely clear if this complex paratextual apparatus is intended to guide the reader − giving him as it were the tone or key to various episodes − or rather to destabilise the reading process, thus impeding the recuperation of the text, that is, its taming or naturalisation by assimilating it to established generic or social models. As always with Stendhal, one suspects that he will have it both ways.

To begin at the beginning, the half-title, as we have seen, purportedly cites Danton: 'The truth, however harsh.' The ramifications of this initial epigraph will help us to test it as a paradigm of the functions served by the epigraphs in general. First, the mention of Danton can be retrospectively assimilated either to the execution motif or to the related Revolutionary motif that runs straight through *The Red and the Black*. A new revolution is what the denizens of the La Mole drawing room most fear, the return of a repressed class that would strip them of their riches and their positions, and plunge France once more into anarchy. That anxiety, however, must never be voiced; though everyone trembles at the thought of it, none dares utter the word lest its very articulation somehow bring it into being. Since every other consideration pales in the face of this one unmentionable fear, the La Mole society is reduced to discussing trivial, inconsequential matters. Whence the boredom from which Julien, and the others as well, suffer in elegant company both in the salon and at the Marquis's table.

When Julien asks if it is a duty or a favour for him to dine everyday with Mme la Marquise, abbé Pirard is scandalised: 'It's a signal honour!' But Julien persists: 'I was less bored in the seminary. I see even Mademoiselle de La Mole yawning some days . . . I beg you, obtain permission for me to dine in some obscure inn for forty sous.' Mathilde overhears this conversation, and it makes her single out Julien for the first time: 'This fellow wasn't born on his knees, like that old priest.' But it is the drawing room, with its regular visitors, its regular activities (ices or tea on the quarter hour; supper and champagne at midnight), its regular backbiting comments and personal mockery, that figures the boredom of nineteenth-century salons, and stands as the flaccid obverse of revolutionary energy. Even its privileged *habitués* 'flee' once the Marquis has retired, and in the following passage,

Stendhal counts on his reader's knowledge of the brilliant and witty eighteenth-century salons to shadow his negative description of the 'bored century' (the entire passage is borrowed from Beaumarchais's *The Marriage of Figaro*):

Provided one did not make light of God, or priests, or the King, or artists protected by the Court, or anything established; provided one said nothing good about Béranger, or opposition newspapers, or Voltaire, or Rousseau, or anyone who speaks his mind; provided, above all, one never spoke of politics, one could freely discuss anything at all.

But forbidden energy breaks out unexpectedly in the social body, like a dormant malady whose symptoms can never be successfully repressed – thoughts of Danton rather than of Rossini dominate the ball in the Hôtel de Retz (II, 8–9). The name of the famous rebel evokes memories of the seventeenth-century Fronde – and thus of energy – but this intimation of vigour is muted or negated by the artificiality of the setting: the courtyard has been beautified to look like a wood of oleander and orange trees, one of the salons is decorated to resemble the Alhambra, and a press of Molièresque *petits marquis* (little aristocrats) proffers fatuous comments on the belles of the ball – 'See, see that gracious smile as she dances alone in the quadrille. It is, upon my honour, inimitable.' In the midst of such frivolity, Mathilde's attention is drawn to Altamira, the political exile who has been sentenced to death in Italy, his own country. The death penalty, she muses, is the only thing in life that cannot be corruptly bought. Overhearing Julien tell Altamira that Danton was a real man, she reflects 'Heavens! could he be a Danton?' Projecting Julien into the role of a Danton cures Mathilde's boredom – like the release of a suppressed impulse – and relieves her from Stendhal's opinion (here voiced by Altamira) that 'There are no more true passions in the nineteenth century; that is why people are so bored in France.' Talk of politics, death, and execution continues to Mathilde's shocked fascination, experienced as a displacement of her own need to participate in a discourse of action. As for her father's secretary,

Julien was supremely happy, unconsciously delighted by the music, the flowers, the beautiful women, the general elegance, and more than anything, by his imagination, which dreamt of distinctions for himself and freedom for all.

The liberal, ecstatic heights to which Julien is raised are completely unaffected by the thought that the ballrooms are in fact filled with conservative enemies (and Altamira makes this point repeatedly) − just as earlier, his joy during the Bray-le-Haut ceremonies was unspoiled by thoughts of the Congrégation: 'In that moment, and in good faith, he would have fought for the Inquisition.'

But what of Danton's epigraph itself? that is, how is the reader to react to a call for the *harsh truth*? The phrase (its attribution, like so many of the epigraphs, is questionable and no doubt waggish) is generally taken to allude to Stendhal's realistic design, the desire to give an authentic fictional portrayal of his age − an aim reinforced by the subtitle, and again by its variant, 'Chronicle of the XIXth Century.' Stendhal's turning to truth in the novel was also encouraged by Tracy's observation on the possibility of reaching truth in that genre.

Although the serious novel of the ordinary life was a creation of the eighteenth century − one can cite Richardson, Marivaux, Prévost, and even Rousseau − the realistic novel is an essentially nineteenth-century phenomenon. The term 'realism', or 'sordid realism', as it was constantly tagged, made its first appearance in a journal of 1826, where it was defined as designating a literary doctrine that 'would lead to the imitation not of artistic masterpieces, but of the originals that nature offers . . .' Realism is linked to the concept of change initiated by the French Revolution. The great events of 1789 disrupted a timeless world of political and moral absolutes (an eternal monarchy and an eternal Church, divinely instituted) authoritatively established by historical continuity. In the minds of many, the world view of mankind was dislocated from the stability of the Universal to the vagaries of the Contingent. Realism ('mimesis') may be considered as an effort to make some sense of that decentring, and is often embodied in the novel of the education of a young man, a novel loosely termed *Bildungsroman*. In France, Stendhal, Balzac, and Flaubert (with *Sentimental Education*) are the chief exponents of this genre. Their novels plot the attempts − half-hearted or enthusiastic, successful or failed − to achieve dominion over new social (and, increasingly, financial) orders.

Yet by seeking to grasp and thus to arrest just such a sense (a new stability), mimesis entangles itself in reproducing an order of what inevitably becomes an authoritarian world ('this is how things are *now*'). This complicity in the alleged establishment of a new social dictate or compulsion has incurred the disapproval of certain modern theoreticians of the discourses of society (of which the novel is one). I shall return to these accusations in chapter 3.

The epigraph in *The Red and the Black* can serve as a guiding Ariadne's thread that will lead the reader into the themes of the work. (See A. Sonnenfeld, 'Romantisme (ou ironie): les épigraphes de *Rouge et Noir*', *Stendhal Club*, 1978). At the same time it plays a mood-setting role; this is what Stendhal seems to have had in mind when he wrote in the margins of his copy of *Armance*, 'The epigraph must increase the reader's sensation or emotion, if emotion there be, and no longer present a more or less philosophical judgement on the situation.' Thus I, 1 of *The Red and the Black*, subtitled 'A small town', bears an epigraph in English ascribed to Hobbes:

> Put thousands together
> Less bad,
> But the cage less gay.

The phrase says approximately this: were society formed of better people, it wouldn't be very lively; that is, the bad side of people is what lends spice to social existence. The chapter then introduces Verrières, gives a history of M. de Rênal's dealings with Père Sorel, and introduces the problem of the tyranny of public opinion in modern republics (the United States) and the French provinces. The 'cage' is the first use of prison imagery, whose tracing out passes through the symbolic retaining walls of M. de Rênal's gardens, the prison inspection, Geronimo's escape story, the seminary, an epigraph attributed to Silvio Pellico (the Italian liberal who was imprisoned in the terrible Austrian prison, the Spielberg, and author of a celebrated prison narrative, *My Prisons*), and finally Julien's cell. The rhetorical variations all revolve about a literary topos and clichéd metaphor, 'life is a prison'. Stendhal's attempt to situate Julien's last days in a liberated space above petty concerns ('your details of real life') is therefore not solely a Romantic fable of the integrated self, but an attempt to evade, to slip out from under the constraints of traditional expression, the *already-saids*, as it were, of imprisoned speech.

The epigraph to I, 2 (and I, 19, 24 and II, 31) is signed Barnave (Speaker of the Assembly) — which brings us back to the Revolution and the guillotine. With the quotation from I, 4 from Machiavelli we are introduced to the suspicions and intriguing nature of the French peasant (Julien's father), triumphant because of his clever use of delaying tactics (*Cunctando restituit rem*: 'Delay puts things right', epigraph of I, 5). Quotations from Byron's *Don Juan* rather obviously (and ironically) preside over the nascent love affair between the 'seducer' Julien and Mme de Rênal. Thus certain epigraphs play a tonal or prefigurative role.

At least two epigraphs find echoes: 'A novel is a mirror that is walked [*qu'on promène*] along a path' (I, 13) is expanded in the celebrated novel definition in II, 19; the epigraph of I, 14 ('A young sixteen-year-old girl had a rosy complexion and she put on rouge') is turned around in its subsequent appearance at the head of Part II ('She isn't pretty, she hasn't any rouge') in order to trigger in the reader's mind a series of ironic contrasts between the book's two parts: Paris vs. the provinces, Mlle de La Mole vs. Mme de Rênal, the artificial vs. Stendhal's *naturel*. An identical quotation from Shakespeare ('O, how this spring of love resembleth/The uncertain glory of an April day') alludes in I, 17 to Julien's lingering mistrust of Mme de Rênal's love, and in II, 19 to Mathilde's mercurial passion (*amour de tête*) for him.

'I obtained advancement, not on account of my merit, but because my master had the gout' (II, 17) is a virtual summary of the chapter it introduces. 'The underground work of the passions' by Mme Goethe (probably a misprint for W. Goethe) epitomises Julien's prison return to love for Mme de Rênal. Schiller, Shakespeare, Mozart, the *Edinburgh Review*, anonymous and phony sources, and a host of greater and lesser luminaries furnish material for Stendhal's epigraphs. They are highly relevant to the text, but they also detach themselves in a gently ironic counterpoint. When Julien has completed his final speech − the 'improvisation' that condemns him in the jury's mind − he moves to an unmarked space, as I suggested above, an *unsayable* realm that is apparently unglossable, for the last four chapters are the only ones in the entire book without epigraphs.

Presages

As we have seen, the epigraphs may play an anticipatory, annunciative role. Danton, the anagram Louis Jenrel, 'my head is lost' (II, 3), the Barnave citations, all predict Julien's death. Other incidents participate in the same proleptic scheme, that is, in the network of presages that foreshadow the bloody outcome. Julien nearly falls under the saw blade in his father's mill, but is saved by the paternal hand; nevertheless, he is 'all bloody' from the blow he has received. Thus his initial fall forebodes the later one under the blade of a guillotine that will not miss. But his isolation and elevation, adumbrations of the prison theme, make their first appearance here also, where we see Julien perched 'five or six feet' above the level of his father and brothers. Blood imagery is frequent in the opening chapters. In addition to this scene, there is, as Julien sets off to report for his job at the Rênal house, the moment in the Verrières church: 'Julien judged that it would serve his hypocrisy to stop in the church.' There he reads the newspaper account of Louis Jenrel's execution and thinks he sees blood near the holy fount. Blood imagery continues in I, 18 ('A King in Verrières'), which, incidentally, opens with a curious anachronism: a displaced excerpt of the Bishop of Agde's chapel homily is cited in the epigraph. The Bishop's address is quoted only later in the chapter, so the epigraph would have to be considered as an 'unpublished' fragment of it. In the chapel are contained the relics of Saint Clement, and a charming statue of the saint:

> He was lying under the altar, wearing the clothing of a young Roman soldier. He had a large wound on his neck, from which his blood seemed to be flowing. The artist had outdone himself; his eyes, dying but full of grace, were half-closed. A budding mustache adorned his charming mouth which, partly open, seemed still to be praying. At this sight the girl next to Julien wept hot tears; one of her tears fell on Julien's hand.

The saint's statue embodies Julien's own double vocation: a religious figure is dressed in soldier's garb; a woman weeps for him; blood flows from his neck. And the candle-lit sanctuary ('more than a thousand votive candles') and procession of twenty or more priests look ahead to Julien's own burial. The inscription on a ribbon calls for Julien's death: 'DEATH TO THE IMPIOUS.'

All the omens of *The Red and the Black* are intended for the reader, and never does Julien experience any intimation of his fate – though he often ponders it. Never does Stendhal engage in the foreshadowing that typically begins with the word 'Later' ('Later he was to realise that . . .'; 'Later, as he walked to the guillotine . . .'), which some novelists employ to whet the reader's appetite. 'Later' phrases are the equivalent of 'to be continued' or 'tune in next week for the exciting finish'. They betoken a certain anxiety regarding the writer's hold over his audience.

Even when Julien is in prison and knows his fate, he does not make retroactive connections. Yet he might have been expected to have some comment for Mathilde about her ancestor and hero, Boniface de La Mole, who suffered the same fate that he is about to meet. This might not offend against *vraisemblance* inasmuch as Julien does think beyond his death, and requests burial in the little grotto near Verrières where he had earlier experienced exalted thoughts of freedom ('Here,' he said, his eyes sparkling with joy, 'men cannot harm me'). Does Julien not suspect that Mathilde, faithful to the history of her race, will project the two of them into the ancestral text? Here Julien, as so often, is a poor reader, in that all these signs or 'texts' remain opaque to him. On the other hand, the Napoleonic text that he knows so intimately is irrelevant to his nineteenth-century situation, having been scripted for another age. The text that Julien fails to read correctly with the gravest consequences is the slanted letter of denunciation that her confessor obliges Mme de Rênal to send to the Marquis de La Mole. Yet it too had an antecedent, in the informer's letter fabricated by Mme de Rênal in order to deceive her husband.

If we question the function of the presage in Stendhal, no one obvious answer stands out. It is a standard practice of his, and we find it reemployed in *The Charterhouse of Parma*. Among the critics, Jean Prévost sees it as a device for bringing the reader closer to the character; for Stephen Gilman, it is a means of exacerbating the very process of reading and of training a 'happy band of Stendhalian readers' (*The Tower as Emblem*, Frankfurt, 1967, p. 25). The presage is certainly a dimension or symptom of authorial control – the advance assignment of a fate – which did not prevent the Existentialists from praising Stendhal's characters for their independence. Julien may ignore his fate, or negligently only half-decipher it, but the reader is never left in doubt by the insistent series of bloody guideposts. Gérard Genette has contended that if the work of verisimilitude in narrative is to 'naturalise' actions (roughly, give them psychological motivation), that *causality* is a part of the realist illusion; for in actuality, the first unit in a fictive temporal order is determined by a second, the second by a third, and so on to the end: 'whence it follows that the last one is the one that commands all the others' (in *Figures II*). Parallel to Sartre's famous analysis of the nature of 'adventures' in *Nausea*, Genette finds that narrative actually is constructed backwards, from effect to cause, from end to means. Since the end was chosen (invented, found) first, this phenomenon is termed the arbitrariness of narrative. At this point we rediscover the literary (fictive) function of the source: the overdetermining, modelling force not of the actual Antoine Berthet's 'story', but of his death. And thus we cannot really speak correctly at all of the phenomenon of *pre*sage, *fore*shadowing, or *ante*cipating of death in *The Red and the Black*, since they do not precede the end, but rather proceed from it. But this is simply the nature of narrative.

The presage leads to reflection on another of the paradoxes or rather the tensions of *The Red and the Black*. The unswerving, predestined, oracularly imposed end of the protagonist aligns it with ancient tragedy or myth (Oedipus being the most famous and relevant): the presage is a manifestation of an unknown but irrepressible desire the character bears within him. Yet this in no way precludes the novel of choice and possibility from opening its own vistas. 'What perspectives,' exclaims Julien in prison, 'Colonel of hussars if we have a war; secretary in a Legation in peacetime; then, ambassador. . . Not exactly, Sir; guillotined in three days' (II, 42). Nor does the narrator, the tracer of Julien's destiny, rule himself out of the game:

He was still very young; but, in my opinion, he was a fine plant. Instead of moving from tenderness to cunning, like most men, age would have given him an easy gift for emotion; he would have been cured of his mad distrust . . . But what good are these vain predictions? (II, 37)

The novel of predictions, then, is constantly tempted to unwrite its own predictions; it practises an unsettled narrativity, cultivates a latent unpredictability.

Narration, irony, and the real

The relation of the Stendhalian narrator to his text is a matter of intense interest, particularly as regards the conventions of realistic fiction. In this connection, it is obvious that Stendhal's practice is far from the self-effacement that Flaubert believed in so strongly. 'Everywhere present, and nowhere visible' was Flaubert's motto for impersonal narration. If this ideal is only imperfectly achieved, even in such acknowledged masterpieces of the realist canon as *Sentimental Education*, narrational invisibility soon established itself as the very hallmark of the story that seemed to tell itself. Two types of fictional narration were postulated on the narrator's presence/absence: 'telling' vs. 'showing', to use Percy Lubbock's phrase (*The Craft of Fiction*, 1929). That is, the novel, like Stendhal's or Balzac's, where the narrator intervenes to comment upon the action, and the novel where the narrator remains in the wings: he stages or dramatises the action, but does not judge it. The absence of a mediating agent was presumed to vouchsafe a higher degree of verisimilitude, for the story would appear to unfold before our very eyes — like life itself.

Stendhal's reader/spectator can never forget that he is hearing a story. Following a tradition inherited from the eighteenth century — and we know that Stendhal had Fielding's *Tom Jones* in mind as he wrote — the narrator intervenes decisively and obviously in his tale. Those intrusions take too many forms to be exhaustively listed, but we may attempt to isolate some of the characteristic forms.

First of all, it is clear that the reading process itself is never a comfortable, passive experience in Stendhal. 'A novel', he writes in *Henry Brulard*, 'is like a bow, and the violin body that makes the sounds is the reader's soul.' Our participation is required, and we are called upon not only to 'follow' the story (make connections, judge, interpret), but to follow the narrator himself: how shall we interpret *his* interpretations?

Very early in the game, Stendhal accustoms his reader to a simple form of irony, such as the liberals' claim — 'but they exaggerate' — that the town trees are severely pruned for abbé Maslon's profit, or the inexperienced Julien's evaluation of Mme de Rênal's age and beauty: 'Julien, who knew all about female beauty, would have sworn at that moment that she was only twenty years old.' Such passages call attention to the narrator just as effectively as those that allude to his alleged personal acquaintance with details of the story's setting ('How often . . . has my gaze plunged into the valley of the Doubs!'; 'What I dislike about the *Cours de la Fidélité* is . . .').

A series of small ironies also attends Julien's success with women. To take only the case of Mme de Rênal: Julien arouses her jealousy quite unwittingly when he learns that M. de Rênal is having all the straw mattresses replaced (I, 9). He begs Mme de Rênal to go quickly to his room, locate a portrait hidden in a box in his mattress, and retrieve it without looking inside. Mme de Rênal complies, thinking the box must contain the picture of Julien's love, whereas Julien is seeking to conceal a quite different passion – for Napoleon. He further increases her amorous concern for him by making an unannounced three-day trip to the mountains, leaving her fraught with anxiety about his decision whether he will stay in the household or accept the imagined rival offer from Valenod. Finally, in the chapter piquantly entitled 'The Cock's Crow' (I, 15), Julien 'seduces' Mme de Rênal by throwing himself at her knees and bursting into tears. (He has similar successes with Mathilde through real or feigned aloofness, and of course by entering into a thoroughly vapid communication with Mme de Fervaques in the episode of the Korasoff correspondence (II, 25–9). Upon returning to his room, he wonders if he played his role well; 'What role?' ironises the narrator; 'the role of a man accustomed to being brilliant with women.'

More complex are what could be termed Stendhal's double ironies, which often have a protective intent. Here the narrator seeks to pre-empt anticipated negative reaction to his characters and their actions. When Julien is carried away by the Bray-le-Haut ceremonies to the point that he would have willingly fought for the Inquisition, or is so impressed by the elegance of the Duke de Retz's ball as to forget that he is surrounded by political enemies, these enthusiasms are not to be understood as damning Julien; rather they demonstrate that he can rise above circumstances to seize joy where he finds it, no matter how unlikely the place. This is the essence of Stendhal's personal system of happiness, *le Beylisme* – 'a practical method of happiness', as Léon Blum called it. As Victor Brombert writes, 'Each poetic idealisation is presented as if it were childish, and yet it never crosses our minds to call his characters' most extravagant acts and wildest dreams

ridiculous or absurd' (*Stendhal et la voie oblique*, p. 162).
Two more examples of double, protective irony are worth
citing.

The first concerns the slowness of Julien and Mme de Rênal
in recognising their mutual love:

In Paris, Julien's position with regard to Mme de Rênal would have
been very quickly simplified; but in Paris, love is the child of novels.
The young tutor and his timid mistress would have found in three
or four novels, and even in the lyrics of the Gymnase, the clarifica-
tion of their position. The novels would have traced for them the
role to play, shown the model to imitate; and sooner or later vanity
would have forced Julien to follow this model, perhaps reluctantly,
and without the slightest pleasure.

In a little town in the Aveyron or the Pyrenees, the slightest incident would have been made decisive by the ardour of the climate.
Beneath our more sombre skies, a poor young man, who is only
ambitious because the refinement of nature makes him need some of
those pleasures that money procures, sees every day a woman of thirty who is sincerely virtuous, occupied with her children, and never
takes examples of conduct from novels. Everything goes slowly,
everything is done little by little in the provinces; life is more natural.

(I, 7)

This passage might be called an example of self-correcting
irony, as well as double irony. It begins with apparent
mockery of slow-witted provincials, who are too unrefined to
have access to the instruments of socialisation (novels) or
culturally deprived (no theatre — the *Gymnase*) to gain insight into an absurdly obvious situation. Yet the oppositive
'but' of the first sentence sets in motion an undercutting of
its disdainful tone and proposition, the social superiority of
Paris over the provinces. The tutor may be 'young'
(= 'green') and his mistress 'timid', and they may not
recognise a situation that countless men and women have lived
before them, yet they would have done so without the
'slightest' pleasure, and unwillingly. At this point the reader
will sense quite confidently that the initial proposition assert-
ing urbanity over provinciality, civility over rusticity, etc., is
subverted, and will want to weigh the connotations of 'role'
and 'model', and perhaps even divine that 'vanity' is the
gravest sin in nineteenth-century society.

The second paragraph might briefly be taken as an emphatic restatement of the first, because of apparent structural parallelisms: just as Paris is superior to the socially untutored provinces in general, so, it would seem, some more 'ardent' provinces are superior to the backward Franche-Comté ('our more sombre skies'). But the passage ends with a clear assertion of provincial advantage and closes on the key term *naturel*, which now allows the reader to recognise in 'role' and 'model' its semantic opposites, and to 'slot' them accordingly. If the 'natural' is a plus, then a 'model' or a 'role' can only be a minus.

A second, purer example of what is called protective irony comes with Julien's invitation to dinner at the Valenod lodgings (I, 22). In the course of the meal the guests can hear the singing of one of the poorhouse inmates. Valenod has him silenced and when Julien observes, 'I don't hear that wretched song any longer,' the director answers, 'I've made the beggars shut up.' This is too much for Julien; despite his 'hypocrisy' (by which Stendhal often means no more than 'self-control'), a large tear trickles down his cheek. 'Happily', no one notices. 'Stop him from singing!' he said to himself. 'Oh God! and you permit it!' Julien then thinks to himself that a good position in his day requires petty chiselling and cruelties of this sort. He yearns for bygone Napoleonic times when fortune resulted from acts of manly heroism. These melancholy reflections are conveyed in a prime example of the many interior monologues that Stendhal's intensely self-analytical characters slip into. (Another example is Mathilde's mulling over of her married future during the ball in Part II.) Then the narrator intervenes:

I admit that the weakness Julien displays in this monologue gives me a poor opinion of him. He would be worthy of being the colleague of those yellow-gloved conspirators who claim to change the whole manner of being of a great country, and don't want to have even a scratch on their consciences.

The passage neatly demonstrates the ambiguity, in the etymological sense of acting in two directions at once, of Stendhalian irony. On one hand, success *does* require compromises − often quite unpleasant ones, as another Stendhalian protagonist, Lucien Leuwen, learns through his symbolic muddying − and the narrator quite properly mocks the tender conscience of Julien the would-be *arriviste* with clean hands. (With Mathilde, Julien will display more advanced reflections on the subject: 'Was Danton right to steal? Should the revolutionaries of Piedmont and Spain have compromised the people by means of crimes? . . . In a word, mademoiselle, ought the man who wants to drive ignorance and crime from the earth pass like a storm and do evil as though by chance?' (II, 9)) Yet, on the other hand, if all action is impure, should conscience therefore be dismissed? Or should not Julien's lachrymosity be admired, as a mark of his integrity? Stendhal will have it both ways, and the reader may simply choose to admire Julien's goodheartedness, deplore his naïveté, or both.

Some ironies probably go undetected by those whose knowledge of Stendhal is limited to *The Red and the Black*. An important example of this type of intertextual (or implicit) irony arises in conjunction with Julien's veneration of Napoleon − a cult not shared by the disenchanted Stendhal:

> For many years, perhaps not an hour in his life had passed without his saying to himself that Bonaparte, a penniless and obscure lieutenant, had made himself master of the world with his sword. This thought consoled him for many misfortunes he deemed great, and doubled joy when it came.   (I, 5)

While a hint of irony is implicit in the disproportion and frequency of Julien's ambition, and more certainly in 'he deemed great', the fully ironic distancing from Julien's chosen model is realised only with knowledge of the key passage from the *Promenades in Rome* that was quoted on p. 12. Napoleon's dazzling success has caused even the young to 'turn their backs on the pleasures of their age'. They remain blind to joy when it is within their grasp. The passage is instructive, for it demonstrates the complex web of relationships all Stendhalian texts entertain with one another, as well as the intimate mixture of autobiography, fiction, and ethnological inquiry characteristic of his writings. The proportions vary from book to book; thus the *Promenades in Rome*, as I have noted, contain a fair number of proto-fictions in the form of anecdotes and other textual raw materials, such as the account of the Lafargue trial. But the point here is that Julien's admiration for Napoleon is misplaced. As F. W. J. Hemmings noted, Julien is practically the sole votary of the Napoleonic cult in *The Red and the Black*, and he learns nothing from the long, cautionary conversation at the beginning of Part II, in which a catalogue of Napoleon's ill-fated influences on French life is drawn up. On the contrary, as we have seen, Julien rushes to visit Malmaison, where 'he wept'.

Julien's tears seem perhaps so ridiculous here that reader reaction is anticipated, and thus brought into the text by means of the protesting voice of an internalised contemporary reader: 'What! despite those ugly white walls constructed this year, that cut the park up into pieces?' 'Yes, sir' – answers the narrator with firmness; and, continuing tongue-in-cheek, 'for Julien, as for posterity, nothing stood between Arcoli, Saint Helena, and Malmaison'. The last comment makes us realise (as part of 'posterity') that we too no doubt share in an uncritical, mystified legend of Napoleonic glory, and are no less exempt from the narrator's gentle twigging than is Julien, or the imagined reader is from his guidance. The passage thus ends in an authorial intervention (I shall return to interventions shortly) of a characteristic sort: it actualises a potentially critical reader reaction (what Victor Brombert called 'the fear of the reader' in Stendhal) in order to disarm it. For although Stendhal may judge Julien's passion misplaced, he is far from condemning passion *per se*. On the contrary, the lack of passion in 1830 France is what he deplores throughout the *Promenades* as well as *The Red and the Black*. Julien's 'follies' – as well as Mathilde's – are proposed for our admiration. As Shoshana Felman has shown, *folie* is an unstable term in Stendhal, very often deployed in favourable contexts. It has an exalting, storybook quality that Stendhal sets in opposition to cold, prosaic reasoning. This much is easily observed in one of *The Red and the Black*'s most celebrated passages (II, 19), one that will take us from irony into narrative interventions.

After her affair with Julien has commenced, a passionate Mathilde attends the opera one evening, only to find herself being projected into the heroine's aria − 'I must punish myself/If I loved him too well' − lines, incidentally, from Cimarosa's opera *Il matrimonio segreto*. She returns home to sing the air over and over at her piano, and the result of her night of 'folly' is that she thinks she has succeeded in conquering her love for Julien. Now Mathilde has as strong a penchant for role-playing as Julien − Marguerite de Navarre and Mme Roland ('O liberty! how many crimes are committed in thy name!') are favourites, even though her female roles do not match up with Julien's male ones. In short, she is just as prone to moments of *folie* as Julien. The narrator once again intervenes out of fear of a certain type of frowning reader, who would point to the 'indecency' of this character, condemned precisely for her folly. The narrator launches into a mock denunciation of Mathilde, alleging that she is purely imaginary, 'and even imagined well outside the social customs which, among all the centuries, will ensure such a distinguished place to the civilisation of the nineteenth century'. (As Christopher Prendergast and Gérard Genette have pointed out, Mathilde's conduct is *unintelligible* in nineteenth-century terms.) Julien, too, is following an implausible line: love alone, without help from a coterie, will not suffice for his advancement. Without a pause, the narrator here challenges his imaginary reader with the famous mirror analogy, expanded from I, 13 where it was attributed to Saint-Réal. (Stendhal, famous for his puckish 'marginal English', may well have engaged in a translinguistic pun here: the Holy Real.)

The passage should be quoted in the original:

Eh, Monsieur, un roman est un miroir qui se promène sur une grande route. Tantôt il reflète à vos yeux l'azur des cieux, tantôt la fange des bourbiers de la route. Et l'homme qui porte le miroir dans sa hotte sera par vous accusé d'être immoral! Son miroir montre la fange, et vous accusez le miroir! Accusez bien plutôt le grand chemin où est le bourbier, et plus encore l'inspecteur des routes qui laisse l'eau croupir et le bourbier se former.

Maintenant qu'il est bien convenu que le caractère de Mathilde est impossible dans notre siècle, non moins prudent que vertueux, je crains moins d'irriter en continuant le récit des folies de cette aimable fille. (II, 19)

Ah, sir, a novel is a mirror walking along the highway. Sometimes it reflects to your eyes the azure of the heavens, sometimes the mire of the road's mudholes. And the man carrying the mirror in his hod will be accused by you of being immoral! His mirror shows the mire, and you accuse the mirror! Instead, blame the high road where the mudhole lies, and even more the inspector of roads who allows the water to gather and the mudhole to form.

Now that it is quite agreed that the character of Mathilde is impossible in our century, no less prudent than virtuous, I am less afraid of causing irritation by continuing with recounting the follies of this amiable girl.

One of the most important aspects of the mirror passage is the phrase *qui se promène*, which I have translated as 'walking' in order to emphasise the mirror's casual objectiveness. To translate *qui se promène* as 'moving along' is perhaps a touch mechanical (Adams; see the discussion of English translations in the *Guide to further reading*). C. K. Scott-Moncrieff's 'carried' and Lloyd Parks's 'being carried', with their passive voice constructions, unfortunately imply a manipulative agent behind the mirror and are at odds with the narrator's point about the mirror's autonomy. One American translation (Charles Tergie; New York, 1961) simply skips the entire passage! Roughly the same concern arises with the word *hotte*. Both Adams and Scott-Moncrieff translate it as 'pack', but how can a mirror carried in a pack 'see'? For this reason, I prefer 'hod', the mason's open tray. The crassness of the real is strongly expressed by the words *fange* and *bourbier* (both repeated), which I have translated 'mire' and 'mudhole'. Most translations clean this passage up and thus attenuate Stendhal's effect by translating 'mire of the puddles' (Scott-Moncrieff) or 'mud and puddles' (Adams). Yet to render *bourbier* by 'puddle' is to efface the matrix concept of mud. Finally, we know that *folie* has a special resonance in Stendhal's idiolect. English 'folly' is certainly an acceptable translation — even though it suggests behaviour madcap rather than mad —

but we should remember that the French word starts from madness, unreason, insanity. Stendhal's vocabulary and phrasings are disarmingly simple and direct, yet are invigorated with private nuances and ironies that are highly challenging.

Indeed, this long intervention, one of the longest in the entire novel, can prove baffling. The narrator ostensibly condemns Mathilde's conduct. Yet the insistent repetition of the word *folie*, used three times, instructs the wary reader that it is not to be taken at face value (and a moral reader would scarcely accept at face value praise for material riches). He terms Mathilde 'imaginary', what would be called 'unrealistic' today. But in the same paragraph the time-honoured metaphor of convincing, life-like representation is adduced. The narrator seems to be saying that Mathilde is imaginary, and Julien is improbable − false − but all the same, let us continue with her story. How is the reader to make sense of such flippancy and contradiction?

With some forcing, this complex passage could be viewed as anticipating a post-modernistic meta-narrative, one that 'lays bare' and deliberately exposes the artifices of story-telling (much as Diderot had done earlier in *Jacques the Fatalist*). Yet within this particular fictional ambit we have already seen that Stendhal set great store by the veracity of the mirror, and deployed the mirror − novel analogy more than once. Thus the narrator cannot be dismissing Mathilde as entirely unintelligible (and Julien with her), for the specular image of natural reflection is immediately brought to the fore in order to exonerate the narrator: don't blame the realistic novelist for what you find in his novels, blame society.

Nor can Mathilde be singled out as the only imagined character. Mme de Rênal is just as exceptional, as *invraisemblable* as Mathilde, if we are to believe in Stendhal as an accurate ethnographer of provincial France. In his book review of *The Red and the Black*, he states that provincial mores (prudery, fear of social contact between the sexes) are the cause of an enormous consumption of novels: 'There is scarcely a single provincial woman who doesn't read five or six volumes a month, and many read fifteen or twenty . . .' Yet Mme de Rênal, alone in this setting, is said never to have read a single novel.

Moreover, the adultery of the *mère de famille* is never condemned by the narrator. Of course she condemns herself, but her Christian piety does not prevent her from placing love for Julien above love for God. The conservative reader whom the narrator so fears pardons (or at least 'reads') Mme de Rênal as a recognised model of female frailty — and more importantly, as a woman who pays for her transgression by her death. Mathilde will not be forgiven her male assumption of desire, that aggressivity which Julien alludes to in prison when he tells her 'Heaven owed it to the glory of your race to have you born a man' (II, 42).

Thus the narrator seems rather engaged in an attempt to forestall a certain type of moral criticism analysed by Gérard Genette in relation to the seventeenth century's objections to *Le Cid* and *The Princess of Clèves*. Corneille's play was condemned on the basis of Chimène's impending marriage to her father's killer. The objections, however, were voiced not in terms of morality, but of plausibility. Chimène offended a certain historical (therefore variable) code of conduct with regard to her passion, but this moral offence was masked behind a discourse of intelligibility: the marriage is at odds with *vraisemblance*, said the critics. In the same way, and with equal vehemence, the Princess of Clèves's confession to her husband that she loves another man was taxed with *invraisemblance*. In both instances an offence to a certain ethical stance was couched in terms of the rational and the natural — a social feature was converted into an unchanging fact of nature.

As Christopher Prendergast writes, 'Desires which are socially problematical, which threaten the social structure (familial in *Le Cid*, class in *The Red and the Black*), are coped with by querying or denying the "plausibility" of the text which presents them' (*The Order of Mimesis*, pp. 122–3). The narrator feigns concession (in a fairly transparent way) to the offended conservative readers of the nineteenth century, for whom Mathilde's passion for her father's servant is unthinkable and offensive.

Stendhal was correct in assuming that they would take

offence. The literary critic Jules Janin, who was to occupy Sainte-Beuve's chair in the French Academy, wrote that 'Mathilde is crazy'. Even Mérimée found Julien 'impossible': 'there is not a single action of his that hasn't contradicted the character I supposed him to have'. To these remonstrances, the narrator has already replied with considerable *disinvoltura*, even insouciance: the mirror reflects by turns behaviours both exalted ('azure') and base ('the mire'). This is the mire. Now that this much is acknowledged, let us get on with the story. That the initiated reader will side with characters who have energy and courage enough ('folly') to brave social convention is a tacit assumption on the narrator's part. Readers attuned to the Stendhalian resonance, 'the happy few' to whom the book is dedicated, would not be interested in lesser characters. Nothing in the narrator's intervention contradicts the myth of Romantic individualism, in which moral superiority is purchased at the price of social integration, or the foregoing of *vraisemblance*, in the petty minds of those with little appreciation for 'singularity' — a key moral term in Stendhal.

The narrator's disavowals of his leading characters are not rare in Stendhal, and the mirror passage (quoted on pp. 42–3) is merely the most celebrated of them. The narrator is critical of the protagonists almost in the same measure that he sympathises with them. He functions as their *alter ego*. Thus while we may properly speak of authorial interventions in *The Red and the Black*, to speak of intrusions would amount to an overstatement of the matter. For the narrator is never an intruder, in the sense of an interloper or an unwelcome presence. Rather he is, as Claude Roy once put it, 'the first and the most admirable of Stendhalian characters' (*Stendhal par lui-même*, p. 54).

But the narrator will also state that he is 'pained' to admit that Mathilde has imprudently exchanged letters with her suitors, and to remark parenthetically of her that such characters 'are fortunately quite rare'; similarly, he dissociates himself fairly frequently from Julien's attitudes of class warfare: 'It must be admitted, the look on Julien's face was atrocious, his expression hideous; it spoke of pure crime. It was the unhappy man at war with all society!' The narrator will intervene to suggest that the reader perhaps shares Julien's boredom with the Fervaques episode, or to praise his conduct ('In my opinion, this is one of the finest traits of his character; a person capable of such self-control can go far, *si fata sinant*' (II, 31)). The narrator calls attention to narrative ellipses (he will skip part of the action), and reintroduces minor characters ('Count Altamira, whom the reader already knows'; 'The reader has probably forgotten the little man of letters named Tanbeau').

That Stendhal takes his aesthetics of the mirror seriously – and that it obliges him to depict even the tedium of reactionary politics – is certainly implicit in the overlong 'Secret Note' episode (II, 21–3), in which royalist conspirators seek to bring about an armed foreign intervention (perhaps led by the Duke of Wellington) to reassert ultra control and restore confiscated forest lands to the clergy. It is rendered explicit in a parenthetical intervention that takes the form of a discussion between the author and his publisher:

(Here the author would have liked to put a page of dots. 'That won't look pretty', says the publisher, 'and for such a frivolous work not to look pretty means death.' 'Politics', the author resumes, 'is a stone tied round the neck of literature, and which sinks it in less than six months. Politics in the midst of imaginative interests is like a pistol shot in the middle of a concert. The noise is deafening without being energetic . . . not in tune with the sound of any of the instruments. Politics is going to give mortal offence to half of the readers, and bore the other half who found it much more interesting and energetic in the morning paper . . .' 'If your characters don't talk politics', resumes the publisher, 'then they are no longer Frenchmen of 1830, and your book is no longer a mirror, as you claim it is.')   (II, 22)

The narrator could at this point have resumed his telling of the secret note in the same insouciant fashion as he did Mathilde's story, with something like 'Now that it has been agreed that politics is unpleasant, let us continue with it'. Instead, for a full account, the narrator refers us to the

Gazette des Tribunaux (a piquant reference indeed, this reference to Stendhal's own source).

It is this very passage that led Erich Auerbach, in his classic study, *Mimesis*, to locate in Stendhal the first expression of a 'modern consciousness of reality', and to state that in *The Red and the Black* 'political conditions are woven into the action in a manner more detailed and more real than had been exhibited in any earlier novel . . .' This is an important point to retain in the face of Stendhal's own alleged apoliticism. It was in *Racine and Shakespeare* that Stendhal had first used his 'pistol in the middle of a concert' image, but then he meant topical political allusions that would soon become obscure. The recycling of the pistol image would therefore seem to confirm the hypothesis that Stendhal viewed the status of his own 'Secret Note' as fragile.

As a final form (and often a cryptic one) of narratorial intervention in *The Red and the Black*, we must cite the foot-notes. Footnotes in fictional works have historically been a device for promoting claims to documentary authenticity, and are found in memoir novels, diary novels, and epistolary novels, particularly of the eighteenth century. The footnotes of *The Red and the Black* are of a more disconcerting sort. In the seminary episode (I, 26), a comparison between Julien's expression and the paintings of Guercino generates a footnote: 'See in the Louvre Museum, François, Duke of Aquitaine, laying down his breastplate and donning a monk's habit (n. 1130).' The effect of this note is highly disruptive to the narrative/fictional pact inasmuch as it refers to an unassimilable, objective reality lying completely beyond any critical attempt to recuperate it, that is, to draw it into the imaginative orbit of the book. It takes us from the world of Stendhal to that of Henri Beyle, 1783–1842, and exposes the book as artifice.

Hardly less jarring is a revolutionary remark uttered at the ball that calls for an editor's note: 'Composed 25 July 1830 [thus before the Revolution], printed 4 August' (II, 8). This note could be assigned to 'Stendhal' (a narrating agent at one remove from the narrator, or a 'heterodiegetic' narrator, to use Genette's terminology), as could the note stating that Julien is a 'Jacobin', and that Altamira is a 'malcontent' (II, 9), and further specifying that this is a footnote by Molière in *Tartuffe*; here the inferred author, like Molière, is moved out of prudence to dissociate himself from a character's utterances (as with Mathilde above). A cryptic note that is entirely personal (back to Henri Beyle) is appended to II, 14: 'Esprit per.pré.gui. II A. 30', for which M. Parturier proposed the following decoding: 'Wit loses prefecture. Guizot, 11 August 1830.' Henri Beyle had requested a prefecture from Guizot shortly after the July Revolution, and wrote to a friend that his petition had been rejected because Guizot wanted no truck with men of wit, 'as I noted in the second volume of *The Red and the Black* . . .' Stendhal apparently wrote his note on a page of proof, and the printer dutifully set it in type. Stendhal is renowned for his marginalia, and no one who knows him well will be surprised at the odd places his graffiti appear, but these are usually handwritten glosses in printed books, not personal codes unintended for a public reader. (There is, however, a comparably sybilline inscription at the end of the Waterloo episode in *The Charterhouse of Parma*.)

Finally, the narrator's last intervention comes *after* the 'finis' of the last page. It is a curious appendage, really more appropriate as a preface. In it he appears to undo all the initial promises of his book. The 'Chronicle of 1830' has been set in an *invented* town, and the author, 'when he needed a bishop, a jury, an assize court, placed them all in Besançon, where he has never been'. But the narrator's last intervention is not Stendhal's last word, for *The Red and the Black* must be complemented by the *Gazette des Tribunaux* trial accounts and the projected book review. In the latter, Stendhal returned to his claims of faithful representation. He termed the seminary episode remarkable for its depiction of manners. The portrayal of the drawing rooms of the aristocratic Faubourg Saint-Germain was 'very true': 'Here M. de Stendhal enters into the depiction of his period.' And Stendhal's word for 'depiction' is *peinture*, literally, 'painting'. At the end of his long review, Stendhal even claims that this novel 'is not one', for 'M. de Stendhal has invented nothing'; it all 'really happened in 1826 near Rennes'. (Of course it all 'really happened' in Stendhal's home province, the Dauphiné, in 1827.) In closing, Stendhal vaunts his originality and daring in painting the mores given to the French by the various regimes that have weighed upon them during the first third of the nineteenth century. One day, this novel will 'depict ancient times the way Walter Scott's do'.

Thus *The Red and the Black* is several texts — and even several novels, if we consider that Mathilde is living according to the romance of her ancestor's life, while Julien is chronicling his own Napoleonic rise. 'My novel is finished, and all the credit is mine', says Julien at the very moment when *The Red and the Black* is propelled beyond its apparent closure by the arrival of Mme de Rênal's letter to the Marquis. This novel cannot be said to end. Its potential for renewal is symbolised in the child, Julien's 'son', that Mathilde will give birth to. Rather, it has stopping points.

To return to one of those points, the authorial claim never to have been in Besançon, we recognise that such passages are precautionary, for Stendhal genuinely feared that he might be prosecuted for the publication of his novel. But for the modern reader, the effect of this narratorial intrusion (the term seems warranted in this instance) — and of the interventions in general — is to problematise the aesthetics of the mirror — novel. Mirrors, we know, are not footnoted; and conversely, words are not mirrors. Through his interventions, Stendhal escapes the potential accusation of indulgence in the referential fallacy, that is, the pretence of offering un-mediated representations of reality — for language does not transmit pure, uncoded reality — nor do stories seam-lessly tell themselves. These narrative indeterminacies are, for Gérard Genette, the essence of the Stendhalian narrator, which is the 'constant and exemplary transgression of the rules and functions apparently constitutive of the literary game'; Stendhal's policy is to be 'always present and always elusive' ('Stendhal', p. 191).

Characters and clashes

Reading, writing, subversion

'Damned bookworm!' Père Sorel's harsh words for his son introduce us to the bookish world of *The Red and the Black*, and the generational conflicts that are staged from its beginning to its end. Julien Sorel is one of world literature's most voracious readers. Reading is the very first activity we see him performing, to the neglect of his assigned duty − watching the saw in the paternal lumber yard. Reading sets Julien apart from his illiterate father, and is the first signal of his radical difference − his 'singularity' − that is confirmed by the physical dissimilarities between the frail Julien, always beaten in boys' games, and his detested older brothers, who 'like giants' mechanically square off trunk after trunk of fir to be cut by the saw. Julien's weak appearance and his slim, supple figure give him a feminine air that further distances him from their male roughness. In fact, when Mme de Rênal first sees him, she mistakes him for 'a young girl in disguise' − a Cherubino-like figure out of one of Stendhal's favourite Mozart operas.

Reading is generalised throughout the novel. With the single exception of Mme de Rênal, every major character could be called a bookworm. Julien has inherited a small library from the old Napoleonic surgeon-major who bequeaths him his Legion of Honour cross, the arrears of his pension, and 'thirty or forty volumes'. Thus the very first of Julien's mentors and surrogate father figures hands down a dual heritage − in the absence of a 'true' father it becomes a virtual heredity − of military glory and of unconventional sociability figured by Napoleon and Jean-Jacques Rousseau. For Julien's favourite book − the one his father sends flying into the stream − is the *Mémorial de Sainte-Hélène*, by Las Casas (a record of Napoleon's life on St Helena and notes on the Emperor's political and historical views by an officer who followed his commander into exile). Julien also favours the *Bulletins de la Grande Armée*, a collection of stirring operational reports issued by Napoleon's general staff. (In *The Life of Henry Brulard*, Stendhal was quick to point out that these bulletins were not accurate historical records, but 'war machines' intended to dupe a gullible public.) But all of Julien's meagre knowledge of the social world is derived from the second great influence on his imagination, Rousseau's *Confessions* – the great autobiographical narrative of another motherless young man's ambitions and adventures, from his early life to 1766. Of notable interest to readers of *The Red and the Black* is Rousseau's love affair with an older woman, Mme de Warens (he was her 'child', and she his '*maman*'), during an intensely happy yet brief pastoral idyll spent at Les Charmettes, a valley to the southeast of Chambéry. There they lived in an atmosphere of Horatian simplicity (Rousseau takes *Hoc erat in votis* as his epigraph: 'This was all I wished for'), and at the beginning of Book VI, he writes:

Here begins the short happiness of my life; now come the untroubled but swift moments that have given me the right to say that I have lived. Precious moments so longed for, ah, begin anew for me your lovely course; flow more slowly in my memory, if you can, than you really did in your fleeting passage.

These pages, as moving today as they were to the Romantic age, are the source of many a poem by Lamartine and Victor Hugo on the dissolution of happiness in time, the tranquillity of pastoral loves far from the great cities of European civilisation, and the discrepancies of memory and reality. Stendhal is not immune to their charms, and Vergy will in retrospect become the *locus amoenus*, the 'happy place' of intimate love that Julien harks back to in the end:

He found a singular happiness when, left completely alone and without fear of interruption, he could abandon himself entirely to the happy days that he had spent in the past at Verrières or Vergy. The slightest incidents of those times, too swiftly flown, had an irresistible charm and vividness for him. Nor did he think of his Parisian successes; they bored him.   (II, 39)

Napoleon vs. Rousseau, the force of willpower vs. tender passion – these are the twin influences at work in Julien's existence; they are the reversing polarities of his story. And yet both are hidden, even repressed adulations, for Julien is afforded few occasions for lyrical, Rousseauist outpourings of his innermost soul, and his cult of Napoleon must be concealed for social reasons, although he makes at least a partial revelation of it to every woman he pays court to, including Mme de Fervaques.

Julien's favourite readings then, his *livres de chevet*, are Napoleon and Rousseau. Yet throughout the novel enough titles are named and authors mentioned to enable us to reconstitute partially his library and his readings. The list is diverse, to say the least: the New Testament, which he has memorised, as well as Joseph de Maistre's *Du pape* (a justification of papal authority); unnamed books his friend Fouqué sends him ('books that he, a theology student, could never ask for in a bookstore'); works of theology (Ligorio); Shakespeare in English; La Fontaine's *Fables*; *La Nouvelle Héloïse*, passages of which he recites from memory to Amanda Binet, Mathilde, and perhaps Mme de Rênal; Rotrou; Molière's *Tartuffe*, another role he has learned by heart; Fénélon; Saint-Simon (the memorialist); Latin authors (Cicero, Horace, Virgil, Tacitus, Martial); Voltaire; abbé Delille; Victor Hugo; Béranger; Scott; military memoirs; and books he has sent from Paris to his prison. He deplores the insipidity of the young men in the La Mole salon who read *René*, the model of Romantic melancholy and *ennui*.

Mathilde de La Mole is the second great reader in *The Red and the Black*, although the Marquis also is a great bibliophile. We first became aware of Mathilde's reading when she surreptitiously enters the library to purloin the second volume of a Voltaire novel. She shares Julien's taste for memoirs and *La Nouvelle Héloïse*, but she also fancies semi-licentious novels. She is particularly fond of chronicles of the energetic sixteenth century, the century of her great ancestor, Boniface de La Mole, and his love, Queen Marguerite. Even the prudish Maréchale de Fervaques, whose choice reading is the genealogical passages in Saint-Simon's *Memoirs*, has read the scandalous *Manon Lescaut*.

Reading is seen by established society as a dangerous, even subversive activity; hence it must be accomplished clandestinely. M. de Rênal flatters himself that he keeps close watch over his servants' reading, and Julien in the seminary is punished for his 'profane' readings, imprudently revealed during his examinations. 'Since Voltaire, since the bi-cameral government, which at bottom is only *distrust and personal judgement*, and gives people's minds the bad habit of *distrusting*, the Church of France seems to have understood that books are its true enemies.' While Julien may shine by his classical readings in the enlightened company at the Bishop's or the Marquis's table, there is no mistaking the surreptitious glee upon his discovery of the great Kehl edition of Voltaire in the La Mole library: 'I shall be able to read all that', he gloats, running to open the library door so no-one can walk in on him unawares. He opens each of the eighty bound volumes. Mathilde, as we have seen, secretly steals books from the library, and she and Julien both disguise their borrowings by spacing the remaining volumes so that no gaps appear. Julien secretly marks books he suspects may interest Mathilde, and indeed they vanish 'for weeks at a time'. In Verrières, in addition to his own inherited books, Julien had access to the abbé Chélan's. Julien receives other books from Fouqué, but dares open them only at night. In a triumph for cerebral enterprise, he often prefers them to Mme de Rênal's nocturnal visits to his room. When he is overwhelmed at the number of books he sees in the Verrières bookstore, which is an unsuitable place for a young theology student to frequent, he must manoeuvre M. de Rênal into taking out a subscription for book rentals under a servant's name. (But ironically, notes the narrator, Julien cannot 'read' the book of Mme de Rênal's heart.)

Finally, as if to prove that the very places of reading threaten the health of good society, and must be quarantined, there is the inner sanctum of the La Mole library. It contains the 'poison' of the most venomous of all books, the 'false *Memoirs*': novels. Though such books are placed under special watch in a little bookcase standing in the Marquis's own bedroom, they are certain to disappear if 'hostile to the interests of the throne and the altar'. Mathilde is Julien's tacit partner in the subversion smuggled in books into the citadel, the castle keep of the establishment. The corrupting influence of novels has infected the Hôtel de La Mole long before Julien makes his appearance there.

The written word, however, is just as threatening to Julien's fortunes as the printed word – and Julien is a proto-writer of sorts, authoring his own 'novel' up to an apparently successful point ('Mon roman est fini'). What he confides to paper is a constant threat to him. The lines written on the back of Napoleon's portrait, his plan for seducing Mme de Rênal, his thoughts in the mountains – all these documents must eventually be obliterated, burned for the most part, as is the case with his biographical sketch of the old surgeon-major. As for the latter document, abbé Pirard (who had earlier discovered the compromising note from Amanda Binet) advises him:

The Marquis does not like scribblers, I warn you; it's his one peeve. Know Latin, Greek if you can, the history of the Egyptians, the Persians, and so on, and he will honour and protect you as a scholar. But don't go and write a single page in French, particularly on important matters above your station in life; he would call you a scribbler and take a dislike to you. What, living in a great nobleman's mansion, you don't know the Duke de Castries's *mot* about D'Alembert and Rousseau? 'That sort wants to argue about everything, and hasn't a thousand écus of income'?

All is found out, thought Julien, here as in the seminary.   (II, 4)

In the case of the secret note (this document too will be destroyed), Julien is of course not so much writer as scribe, and he is a mere copyist of the Korasoff correspondence with Mme de Fervaques. As Christopher Prendergast has pointed out, this exchange succeeds precisely to the degree that it is 'empty' (London and Richmond are perfectly inter-changeable with Paris and Saint-Cloud); it is a perfect model of safe writing. 'Failures' in Julien's writings spread across the comic range from *cella* to cuckold ribaldry (his counter-feit poison pen letter concocted for M. de Rênal), and the elaborately mystified: the account of his affair with

Mathilde, written in story form (*conte*), and packaged with Mathilde's compromising letters in a series of Protestant Bibles expressed to Fouqué with secret instructions to publish them in the event of his death in suspicious circumstances. It is finally, of course, an irony that a virtually forged letter from Mme de Rênal should expose Julien, and 'close the book' on him, as we are told by the running head of the page where he fires on her in church. Julien's misadventures stem, in a very real sense, from failures in reading and writing. He does not properly assess the relevance of the texts he reads to the text of his own life (the model of the Napoleonic age is inappropriate), nor can he bring his own novel to a successful term. With his final letter to Mathilde, Julien abjures writing and seeks to move beyond both speaking and writing in the assumption of a new, *other* language, a Romantic purity lying beyond signs and which is figured by an alien sign system, his quotation from Shakespeare (his only use of English): 'From this time forth I never will speak word' (II, 36).

Ambition and imagination

We have seen that Bonaparte's phenomenal rise from artillery lieutenant to master of Europe has stimulated and coloured one aspect of Julien's imagination that invariably makes for uneasy reader reaction: his ambition. Ambition is the motor of his rise (M. Bardèche termed *The Red and the Black* an 'ascensional novel'), and is thus inseparable from his energy. Energy is clearly prized in the novel's value system; its absence from Paris and from the bloodless nineteenth century in general is repeatedly deplored and unfavourably contrasted with Julien's and Mathilde's models. Yet the narrator twice speaks of Julien's 'black ambition'; ambition energises but, concomitantly, it distorts. These distortions are inseparable from the work of the imagination. Whereas a coldly ambitious character could be expected never to be deflected from a vision of the world of facts, the imagination blurs the view of the-way-things-are. Julien falls prey to moments of enthusiasm when he might least be expected to do so: at the ball in Paris, at the Bray-le-Haut ceremonies when he would have fought for the Inquisition. The tolling of the church bells for the Corpus Christi procession in Besançon is most instructive. It moves Julien deeply: 'His imagination was no longer on earth.' The narrator intervenes to state that he should rather have been thinking about cutting the cost of the bell-ringers by paying them off in indulgences; instead, Julien's soul, 'exalted by these virile and ample sounds, was roaming through imaginary realms. Never will he make a good priest, nor a great administrator. Souls so moved are good at most for producing an artist.' (But the artist-writer in Julien will not come to fruition either.) What is so often apparently deplored in interventions of this nature, as we have seen, is here actually favoured. For in 'Beylism', what the rational self ought to find incompatible with personal and political beliefs is not allowed to intrude upon moments of happiness, whatever the source. As F. W. J. Hemmings has written, imagination is the morally purifying element in Julien.

Support for this claim can be seen in the notes Stendhal jotted down for a story he sketched out several years after the publication of *The Red and the Black*. He called the story 'A.-Imagination', by which he designated a character thoroughly lacking imagination. This personage, Robert, was conceived as a counter-Julien. 'The author', wrote Stendhal, 'ten years ago sought to create a tender and honest young man; in Julien Sorel he made him ambitious, but still filled with imagination and illusion. He intends to make Robert completely without imagination other than what helps him to invent schemes to arrive at a fortune.' Robert is an out-and-out rascal. He is wooing a rich widow. When a rival in love with her challenges him to a duel, Robert proposes a deal: 'Give me a hundred thousand francs, and I'll make her dislike me.' One sentence epitomises Robert: 'Never is his opera glass obscured by the breath of imagination.' Thus for Stendhal the lack of imagination is damning. But if imagination is a redemptive element, as we have seen, it exposes the Stendhalian characters and makes them prey to misunderstandings of their own qualities. This Stendhal calls 'inverted imagination'. When Julien is at his unhappiest with Mathilde, thinking she loves one of the young noblemen of her father's drawing room, he deprecates all his own qualities: 'in this state of *inverted imagination* he undertook to judge life with his imagination. This error is that of a superior man' (II, 19). (Mathilde might be said to suffer from 'inverted pride'; when writing to her father, she takes a perverse pleasure in styling herself 'Madame Sorel, daughter-in-law of a Verrières carpenter'.)

Thus ambition and imagination model one another, and do so nowhere more iconically than in the scene of the young Bishop of Agde rehearsing his gestures (I, 18). Too young for his position, the Bishop practises his new role before a full-length mirror, by giving innumerable gestures of benediction and looking older than his age. The mirror is significantly called a *psyche*. The sight of such youthful success restimulates Julien's ambition. Forgetting Napoleon and military glory, he thinks: 'So young and Bishop of Agde! but where is Agde? and how much is it worth? two or three hundred thousand francs perhaps.' This is actually one of the few times Julien is seen making money calculations, despite his early expressed desire to 'make a fortune'. This desire too escapes baseness through its relation to a form of delicacy — the young peasant wishes to escape the brutal family milieu he was raised in, and is 'only ambitious because the refinement of his nature makes him feel a need for some of the pleasures that money gives . . .' Antoine Berthet might have been speaking for Julien when he aspired to a status above that of 'a magister with 200 francs of wages'.

Money, or the too obvious love of it, is a well-traced moral fault line in *The Red and the Black*. The repellent characters — M. de Rênal, Valenod, Julien's father — are money-grubbers to a man. Julien's successful salary negotiations with M. de Rênal are all accomplished in spite of himself, and he refuses to take a cut of one of the Marquis's bond market operations. Money matters, integral to the realism of Balzac, are wholly uncongenial to the Stendhalian universe. So seldom does he attend to money that it is only by a stroke of inspiration that the imprisoned Julien deflects all his father's reproaches with a single phrase: '*I have savings*!' Julien is no vulgar fortune hunter; had he been no more than this, he could have accepted Fouqué's offer of association in his thriving timber business, or even pursued Prince Korasoff's offer to arrange a marriage with his cousin, a 'rich heiress'. Money then, is not the form that Julien's ambition assumes. The Marquis, while conceding that Julien does not have the scheming character 'of a Louis XI', has some suspicions regarding this motive, though, and thus he is moved to write to Mme de Rênal. Her allegation that seeks to seduce the lady of the house (using 'phrases from novels') necessarily hits home, but we can guess that her second, related accusation most outrages Julien because it is at one and the same time plausible and utterly false: 'Poor and avaricious . . . his main and sole object is to succeed in gaining control over the master of the house and his fortune.' As Julien well knows, Mme de Rênal (and Mathilde, to whom he has confided his ambition) knows better − yet he fails properly to decipher this, the last of a series of unintelligible, cryptic texts going back to the newspaper scrap in the church. Here the book closes, the novel of the parvenu is 'finished'.

Now the 180 steps he climbs to a state of grace far from the eyes of men lead him to formulate exactly the fortune to which he aspires: 'Two or three thousand livres of income to live peacefully in a mountain area like Vergy . . . I was happy then . . . I didn't realise my own happiness!' 'When he was ambitious', the narrator comments, 'not to succeed was the only shame in his eyes.'

Masks

Before attaining the moral and material height of serenity and strength, Julien makes many a detour. The concealment of his ambition leads Julien of necessity to practise hypocrisy − etymologically related to role-playing − for that is the art of the weak. 'Alas', he sighs, 'it is my only weapon!' But it is not easy for him to play the hypocrite incessantly, nor should his memorising of Tartuffe's role mislead us on this score. Julien's roles are trials of strength to be endured in the face of a variety of challenges: the hostility of his companions in the seminary, the excruciating boredom of the La Mole salon, the vapidity of the laboriously copied Korasoff correspondence. Perhaps only Mathilde can appreciate the extent of Julien's self-control in such circumstances. (Her own opinions in the garden differ a great deal from those she subscribes to in the drawing room.) Listening to Julien's conversations with the Maréchale de Fervaques, in which he constantly professes the opposite of what she knows to be his true opinions, she is struck by his 'Machiavellianism', little suspecting that he has undertaken this role precisely in order to regain her love: 'His efforts to play a role were succeeding in robbing him of all strength of soul.' As John Mitchell remarks, 'it never occurs to him that Mme de Fervaques is precisely the person he should cultivate in order to advance not his love-life, but his career . . .' (*Stendhal: Le Rouge et le Noir*, p. 35).

Reading and role-playing may be connected. Julien comes late to the realisation that one's social gestures constitute the self into a signifying system that produces meaning: one is a text for others. Julien finds himself too easily 'read' by Abbé Chélan when he turns down Elisa's marriage proposal; his refusal does not, as he intended, give the priest a good opinion of his own priestly vocation. The abbé detects rather in Julien what he calles a 'sombre ardour' (which Julien inwardly identifies as his 'plan to make my fortune'), and thus sees through his mask. Julien concludes, as a disciple of the *Idéologues* might have done, that henceforth he must rely on 'the tested parts of my character'. Three days later, Julien returns with his pretext for refusing Elisa, and it is indeed a 'story' (a text), in fact a lie. Elisa, he insinuates to the abbé, is impure. The narrator apparently is far from being disturbed at Julien's calumny; on the contrary, he dismisses his character's misconduct, and even congratulates him, stating that Julien will fabricate even more convincing social roles once he has been exposed to the proper models. But 'model' is a term previously encountered in the narrator's private vocabulary as a negative term. This praise of Julien will be read ironically, as wry or mock praise, and all this is much in keeping with Stendhal's games of irony and double irony.

But if he seems to place the model and the natural, Paris

and the provinces, Don Juan and Werther, society and the individual, Mathilde and Mme de Rênal, words and silence, into pairs of opposites, we must not conclude too hastily that one of the terms stands for the authentic and the other for the false. The frontiers between the terms are highly unstable, and the mask, or social text, should be viewed as a moral no-man's-land, a testing ground that mediates between self and society in the striving for a synthesis yielding a new truth. As Michel Crouzet writes, 'all truth passes through travesty' (*Stendhal et le langage*, p. 65). But irony is also an indication of Stendhal's own unresolved attitude toward his protagonist. As Elizabeth Tenenbaum has noted, Stendhal admires both the sensitive, spontaneous Julien, and the rational, self-disciplined Julien (*The Problematic Self*, p. 50). And already in 1914, in his famous book on *Stendhal et le beylisme*, Léon Blum had signalled the paradox of the *voluntary* pursuit of a happiness that cannot be willed.

Even the most natural character of the novel, Mme de Rênal, plays roles and finds great personal delight in doing so. She, who has never read novels and so is without models to deform her conduct, nevertheless permits herself 'the delicious sensation' of pleading Elisa's cause with Julien. For an hour, in a highly staged, Marivaux-like scene (I, 8), she hears her rival's hand and fortune constantly rejected. And it is precisely because she took on this role of (false) mediator − of go-between − that she arrives at her own harsh truth, the knowledge that she loves Julien. The mask has thus removed her from feint to fact, and Stendhal has recourse to the following metaphor to describe her discovery: it is a 'singular spectacle'. The secret truth of the self cannot be separated from acting, which leads to self-possession: 'Somewhat adroit since she had fallen in love, she explained her colour [upon hearing Julien's voice] as a terrible head-ache.' Thus are dissimulation and self-discovery implicated in the guilty game of self-discovery in love.

Duty

Julien's self-control, his much exaggerated 'hypocrisy', is perhaps best evaluated within the context of his *devoir* ('duty'), a complex set of self-imposed constraints. Julien's duty is a continuing test of his willpower, undertaken in order to overcome fear or to satisfy his pride. Conceived as acts of courage, they naturally assume a military cover. '*Aux armes!*' he cries to himself when he hesitates before the gate of the Rênal household. The most celebrated episode of his *devoir* is the seizing of Mme de Rênal's hand by ten o'clock, failing which he vows to return to his room and blow his brains out. The comical struggle that ensues over her hand is resolved in his favour, and he is overcome with happiness, 'not that he loved Mme de Rênal, but a horrible torture had ceased'. The next day he has scarcely a thought for her. 'He had done *his duty, and a heroic duty*.' He is so pleased with himself that he locks himself in his room to reread the *Bulletins de la Grande Armée*. Militarily exploiting his advantage, he decides he must 'tell that woman that I love her' — although he would prefer to pay court to her companion Mme Derville, who has never seen him in his low position as a sawmill hand: 'I must have one of these two women.'

Here a narratorial intervention makes a noticeably ironic use of *duty*: mocking Julien's calculating approach to love, it states that without abandon (*laisser-aller*) 'love is only the most tedious of duties'. Such interventions leave the reader in little doubt as to the narrator's opinion of Julien's campaign; and this one is followed up by a reference to Julien's 'petty vanity' and a denunciation of his failure to live 'day by day', an ideal he will realise only in prison. Julien's 'victory' — his trembling journey through the château corridors at two in the morning, his falling at Mme de Rênal's feet, his bursting into tears — all these are to be read not only as a satirical repudiation of his self-image as a seducer, but against its intertextual other, the Viscount de Valmont's diabolical novel of sexual duplicity, *Dangerous Liaisons* (1782). Moreover, Julien's duty spoils his pleasure; afterwards he can only worry whether he played his part to satisfaction. 'What role?' he asks the narrator, who immediately supplies the answer: 'The one of a man accustomed to being brilliant with women.' Thus the 'seduction' of Mme de Rênal figures the gap of inauthenticity in Julien, separating self and copy. The psychological bridging of that gap is in an important sense nearly the whole of 'Julien's story.'

Yet, once more, each moral characteristic in Stendhal's universe has its obverse. If Julien's *devoir* misleads him, it also guides him in nearly equal measure. In prison, when he can at last make a valid assessment of his existence, he acclaims it as a 'powerful idea', and compares it to a solid tree trunk during the storm. The 'iron hand of duty' serves him well during his combat with Mathilde (where we see the link between duty and hypocrisy), and as might be anticipated, Mathilde herself is prone to just as chimerical and imperious a sense of duty as Julien. In her nascent love for him she tells herself that 'All must be singular in the fate of a girl like me'; and aristocratic arrogance bolsters her self-reliance. Pride in her lineage, particularly her heroic ancestor, Boniface de La Mole, is what enables her to recognise in Julien a steeliness unobservable in the young gentlemen of her entourage who, were a new revolution to break out, would display great dignity on their way to the guillotine ('heroic sheep', she calls them). It is Mathilde's personal duty to be 'singular'. This duel of prides augurs ill for their love.

Julien's duty also consists of a prickly sense of personal honour. The eagerness with which he demands satisfaction in Paris (which leads to his duel with the Chevalier de Beauvoisis) harks back to Besançon, when Julien reluctantly backed down from a possible confrontation with one of Amanda Binet's suitors, at her insistence. Both incidents rankle with Julien because they took place in a café: they were experienced as public humiliations. At his trial, Julien spies an insolent look from Valenod (one of the jurors); the thought of being scorned by the parvenu Baron (new mayor of Verrières, and contemptible former director of the poorhouse) spurs his decision to address the jury: 'My horror of contempt . . . causes me to speak.' He then braves the bourgeois jurors, insisting that his crime is of a social and not a political nature, and was fully premeditated. He forecloses the possible *crime passionnel* defence, and issues a thundering defiance of class privilege.

Julien thus has a nearly Spanish sense of pride. He refuses to eat with the Rênal servants. 'I am little, but I am not base', he explodes at Mme de Rênal's offer of some money for underclothing. Chafing under M. de Rênal reproaches, he tells him 'I can live without you, sir'. In Paris, people are too polite to scorn him openly. As Abbé Pirard takes care to explain to the Marquis: 'This young man, although low born, has a proud heart, and he will be useless to you if his pride is offended; you would only make him stupid.'

L'imprévu

Julien's pride, related of course to his ferocious sense of independence, makes him 'unreadable' on many occasions to social conventionalists. It introduces us to another term mapping the moral fault lines of *The Red and the Black*. This is *imprévu* − the 'unforeseen' and the unforeseeable in the conduct and reactions of one who, paradoxically, is at times viewed as hypocritical and scheming. *Imprévu* is a cleavage word in Stendhal. Julien possesses it; it charms Mme de Rênal. It offends two of the most socially conservative characters in the book, the Marquise de La Mole and the Maréchale de Fervaques. In the latter, its absence becomes

the impossibility of any live emotion. The unforeseen in one's actions, the want of self-control would have scandalised Mme de Fervaques almost as much as the absence of dignity toward one's inferiors. The slightest sign of sensibility would have been in her eyes a sort of *moral intoxication* to blush over, and which was highly damaging to what a person of high rank owes to herself. (II, 26)

One can see quite clearly here a definition of 'what one owes onself' − one's duty − that is entirely the opposite of Julien's moral autonomy. And for the Marquis de La Mole, *imprévu* is the 'horror of great ladies': it is the antipode of 'what is proper'.

The Marquis, however, takes Julien's side; he is less respectful of convention than his wife, and boredom actually leads him to suspend the rules of social hierarchy and to receive Julien on equal footing. In Julien he finds *imprévu* – something his own son lacks – and this justifies awarding him the Legion of Honour. *Imprévu*, then, is a spontaneity that is the very nature of the threat to the aristocratic order. The unpremeditated cannot be incorporated within the rules, and by receiving Julien in his blue suit (see below, p. 75), the Marquis allows himself just as dangerous an act as receiving the 'venom' of novels in his bedchamber. *Imprévu* is allied to the imagination to the extent that it is uncalculating.

Mathilde, who thrills to the imagination just as much as Julien, is all aquiver at Julien's seizing of the medieval sword (kept in the library 'as a curiosity'); thinking herself transported to the times of the heroic aristocracy when ladies might stab or be stabbed by their lovers, she tells herself, in astonishment and rapture, 'Thus I was about to be killed by my lover!' On the personal level, *imprévu* is incompatible with the skilled approach to human affairs. Had Julien walked in the garden after this incident, writes the narrator, Mathilde would have found a way to make it up with him – but such artfulness would not admit the 'sublime' gesture of unsheathing the sword in the first place.

Finally, *imprévu* becomes a key term in the Marquis's desire to learn if Julien is an exploitative *arriviste*: 'Was there true, spontaneous love? or rather the vulgar desire to raise himself to a fine position?' As Christopher Prendergast writes, *imprévu* is the mark of the way that Julien 'repeatedly eludes and disturbs the "internalised probability system" of the other characters' (*The Order of Mimesis*, p. 124). The reader is made to feel, moreover, that the imaginative and the unpredictable elements in Julien are more instinctively his than the acquired social traits of ambition and hypocrisy. Thus Julien in prison can forgive himself for his ambition. There is indeed no more room for it once he has accepted the imminence of his death and decided to live not for others (the source of hypocrisy), but 'for the day'. As ambition necessarily includes the future, it vanishes with the acceptance of a day-to-day existence.

Singularity and solitude

Yet another remarkable and related characteristic of Julien's moral make-up must be considered, one that is commented upon by many of the other characters, and to which the narrator constantly calls our attention: his *singularity*. 'Singular being' is the epithet often used to designate Julien, and 'singular' is an adjective used more than half a dozen times to describe some aspect of his comportment. 'Tempestuous' is also appropriate for one possessed of what the narrator calls 'the sacred fire'. That sacred fire is described in *De l'Amour* (chapter 25), where it is given as the 'source of the passions'. It is another of those decentring qualities that throws Stendhalian souls into a lively, passionate response to the world, and by the same token causes them to assess it inaccurately. Mathilde is also endowed with the sacred fire, according to her suitor, M. de Croisenois, who is not at all appreciative of his intended's unconventionality. Her behaviour, too, is viewed in her circle as 'singular'. She herself applies the term to her adventure with Julien: 'Everything must be singular in the destiny of a girl like me.'

The sacred fire of enthusiasm is redemptive of the very errors the 'a-imaginative' Robert would never fall victim to. Singularity, then, is yet another of those touchstones of moral authenticity; yet as it elevates Julien and Mathilde in this ethical sense, on the social level and in the society of nineteenth-century France it sets them apart, making them objects of suspicion, and even hatred. This is particularly true in the closed, secretive world of the seminary where Julien discovers for himself the maxim that 'difference engenders hatred', and where Abbé Pirard sees in him 'something that offends the vulgar'. Here we touch upon a specifically Romantic character, the outsider, the social misfit, the *homme fatal*, set apart from the common run of mortals by some terrible, even frightening otherness. (M. de La Mole finds Julien brilliant,

but deep in his character also finds 'something frightening.')
At the seminary, Julien's fellow seminarians ostracise him
with a rebel's name, 'Martin Luther'.)

Aside from Fouqué, Julien makes no friends. In Paris, all
his acquaintances drift away after six weeks, and he has difficulty finding someone to serve as his second during his duel.
And singularity even marks Julien's entombment: the in-
habitants of small mountain villages are attracted by the
'singularity of this strange procession'. 'Singular', in the
social context, means no more than *bizarre*. Yet for the
Romantic individualist it is the outward sign of an indispensable uniqueness, an unsocialised independence. For these very
reasons there is a great ironic contradiction in Julien's
incautious admiration for any model — still less for a model
of authoritarianism called Napoleon.

The singularity that sets Stendhalian characters apart also
leaves them alone, with a marked taste for solitude. Solitude
is the condition accompanying singularity, the overt rejection
of the social, and thus the contemplation of inner resources
and the domain of the self. (The Romantic self, as I have
already indicated, constitutes an antecedent authenticity, a
unitary subject preexisting society.) 'Mr Myself' gestures
toward this site of authentic self-knowledge and self-
sufficiency. Romantic solitude is a Rousseauist heritage, and
a literary cliché by the time it reaches Stendhal. Yet perhaps
no writer has given a more striking symbolisation of the myth
in European fiction. In his two great novels the treatment of
solitude is imaged in the protagonist's elevation (Proust was
one of the first readers to call attention to Stendhal's predilection for the 'high places'), and isolation in the theme of the
happy prison.

Prison

Both Julien and Fabrice del Dongo (hero of *The Charterhouse of Parma*) find unexpected happiness in their incarcera-
tion. 'Can this be a prison?' exclaims the rapt Fabrice; and
Julien, with a sense of the comic his creator does not always

receive full marks for, wryly complains that the only drawback to prison is that one can't escape visitors. All the truly Stendhalian characters seek solitude, which becomes another of those moral cleavages dividing the *sympathiques* from the *antipathiques*, and making them just as easily recognisable as a Hollywood Western's white hats and black hats. Long moments of solitude are unbearable to a woman of Mme de La Mole's rank. In her eyes, 'solitude is atrocious: it is the emble of *disgrace*'. Mme de Rênal, on the other hand, finds deep enjoyment in solitude, and even those who flee the small-mindedness of provincial life (ruined by the petty persecutions of the Congrégation, like Falcoz and Saint-Giraud), maintain a nostalgic view of what country life used to be. 'O countryside, when shall I see thee' is the ironic, mockingly Virgilian epigraph to this farewell to a bucolic state of well-being. In fact, the structural opposition of the novel (Part I, *la Province*; Part II, Paris) underscores the latent pastoral appeal for a forfeited innocence and forth-rightness that subtends *The Red and the Black*. That serenity is recovered *in extremis*, in a radical rejection of and rebellion against every form or vestige of the social contract, in an attempt to transcend even language. The entrance into silence is the unfigurable beckoning to that realm. Solitude is the necessary prelude to, or antechamber of, a state of grace or self-sufficiency. Julien experiences its appeal most strongly, and although he gives it its most poetic expression once he is imprisoned, he has an early premonition of its happiness in Vergy after he has left the place that retrospectively takes on an Edenic colouring in his mind:

One thing astonished Julien: the solitary weeks spent in Verrières, in M. de Rênal's house, had been a time of happiness for him. He had encountered feelings of revulsion and melancholy thoughts only in the dinners that had been organised for him; in that solitary house, was he not free to read, write, and meditate without being disturbed? He was not torn away at every moment from his brilliant reveries by the cruel necessity of studying the movements of a base soul [i.e. Valenod], and what is more, to deceive that soul by hypocritical words or actions.

Could happiness be so close to me?   (I, 23)

Hundreds of pages later, Julien will answer his own questions: 'Then I was not aware of my happiness.' Julien's happiness, like Mme de Rênal's (in the phrase applied to both of them), must be forged 'far from the eyes of men'.

The high places of predilection are Julien's tall rock, a physical vantage point and a place of moral superiority from which his view embraces miles of territory as a sparrowhawk circles silently overhead, and the grotto where he writes his thoughts and where he is eventually buried. But Vergy, the paradise lost of the retrospective imagination, is also a mountain place. There Mme de Rênal experienced the existential pleasure, the *presence* of being in love ('elle se laissait vivre'), in absorbing the deep contentment of her natural surroundings: the wind rustling in the lime trees, the first drops of rain striking the leaves, the sweetness of the darkness. And just before his death, Julien participates in this same ravishing simplicity: 'In the past', Julien tells Mme de Rênal, 'when I could have been so happy during our walks in the woods of Vergy, a burning ambition led my soul into imaginary lands. Instead of pressing to my heart this lovely arm that was so near my lips, the thought of the future took me away from you.' In the privileged prison space, solitude is a celebration of difference, of apartness and singularity. There the self is known as a serenity deriving from freedom from Others and from Social Opinion ('your petty affairs'). Julien dies, yet in his private terms he prevails. If he can no longer triumph, no longer conduct 'his novel' to a successful end by worldly reckoning, he can at least avoid defeat and exit the world unvanquished — like 'Danton, Mirabeau, and Carnot, who knew how not to be defeated'. The implications of this phrase, with its nearly Nietzschean ring, are made clearer when Julien receives the visit of the aged and nearly crippled Abbe Chélan:

If I expected to die in bed, then the sight of that poor old man ought to make me feel wretched; but a swift death, in the flower of my years, is just the thing to spare me that sad decrepitude.

Julien, then, will avoid submission to the 'shipwreck of old age', to use Charles de Gaulle's metaphor. He will also elude the callousing of the spirit that age brings. This, Jean Prévost wrote, is Stendhal's true reprieval, the ultimate boon he bestows upon his dearest creations, a form of 'literary euthanasia' (*La Création chez Stendhal*, p. 260). Like some Malraux hero seeking to *mourir très haut* ('to die a noble death'), Julien seeks above all to avoid the weakness of decline. He is turned definitively towards the past, and towards the simple happiness that Vergy stands for in hindsight. This is Stendhal's poetics of the sublime, a poetics that traditionally is marked by stylistic simplicity, by the 'zero degree' of rhetoricity.

Style

Stendhal, a severe critic of the mellifluous style that Chateaubriand epitomised for him, always sought to write 'below' a certain level of Romantic bombast. In this respect, we may cite *De l'Amour* (ch. 9) — in fact to cite it in its entirety is to give the reader a good idea of what is meant by the simplicity of the sublime:

> I make every possible effort to be *dry*. I want to impose silence on my heart, which thinks it has a lot to say. I'm always fearful of having written only a sigh, when I think I've noted a truth.

Yet Stendhal was highly critical of this dryness of style. In a letter to his editor (November 1835) he criticised *The Red and the Black* for its 'choppy' style, and his own marginal notations on a personal copy of the novel (known as the Bucci copy) deplored his writing, finding it 'abrupt, halting, jerky, harsh'. Rereading his description of the denizens of the La Mole drawing room, Stendhal promises himself to add descriptive detail and the 'picturesque part' for a second edition. Without these 'three or four descriptive words per page, much of this sounds like a moral treatise'. 'Horror of modern blather had thrown me into the opposite fault: dryness of several parts of *The Red and the Black*. Now and then, a line of description, of physical movement would aid comprehension a great deal.' Nathalie Sarraute has neatly summed up the unadorned Stendhalian style: 'a dry style, direct, perfectly natural, as if it goes without saying, free from all redundancy, shorn of affectation, stripped to the extreme, transparent, invisible' (*Preuves*, February 1965).

Style, of the sort Stendhal admired, comes up for consideration in the episode of the Korasoff correspondence, Julien's letter-writing campaign to win the esteem of the Maréchale de Fervaques and recapture Mathilde's love. (The Julien – Mathilde – Mme de Fervaques triangle provides one of the illustrations for René Girard's concept of the *mediated* nature of desire (*Deceit, Desire, and the Novel*, pp. 6–7). As the Maréchale clearly falls to the wrong side of those moral fault lines separating Stendhal's characters, it is significant that she actually admires the length of the phrases she receives from Julien: 'It is not the jerky style popularised by Voltaire, that immoral man.' The use of 'jerky' by this personage is instructive: it is not to be condemned altogether as a stylistic flaw, despite Stendhal's self-criticism.

Gérard Genette ('Stendhal', p. 182) quotes from Stendhal's *Marginalia* (II, 96) an enlightening comparison that Stendhal made between his own style and Mérimée's. In the following brief passage, 'Clara' is Mérimée, and 'Dominique' is one of Beyle's favourite pseudonyms:

'He made her dismount, using a pretext', Clara would say. Dominique says: 'He made her dismount by pretending to see that the horse was losing one of its shoes and that he wanted to fix it with a nail.'

Stendhal's sense of realism, of respect for the 'small true fact', causes him to add anchoring details that Mérimée finds unnecessary. Yet such respect for detail does not conflict with Stendhal's professed admiration for a no-nonsense style, such as that of the civil code. To feel like Rousseau *and* to write like Montesquieu (lucidly and to the point) was his literary ideal.

To return to the sublime: it is, as Genette explains, not a *less* ornamented style, but rather a style more simply ornamented, and well attested to in Classical manuals of rhetoric (*Figures*,

p. 208). The sublime — the top of the stylistic register — is thus identified by a virtual blank. (This can be considered a Neo-classical trait as well, recognised in the terseness of Pascal's aphorism, 'True eloquence mocks eloquence.') Thus the plenitude of Julien's existence is figured by seemingly paradoxical phrasings. In prison, he leads a life paradoxically full of a *lack*: 'a life full of *incurie* [lack of cares] and tender reveries'. Julien's rejection of *Others* (italicised in the text) is the sign that he has achieved an integration of the self that is nearly a state of pure desire, of unmediated desire. The telescoping of Julien's last moments is revealing in its juxtaposition of death and desire: 'The sweetest moments that he had known in the past in the woods of Vergy came crowding into his mind with an extreme energy.'

Stendhal's directness is another marked stylistic feature. 'Let us be Classical in our expressions and turns of speech' (*Racine and Shakespeare*, X); 'The best style is the one that makes itself forgotten and allows the thoughts it utters to be most clearly seen' (*Memoirs of a Tourist*); 'I see only one rule: style cannot be too clear or simple' (Letter to Balzac, 16 October 1840). In this same letter to his famous contemporary, Stendhal affirmed that the importance placed upon form in art was lessening each day. Here he was quite mistaken, for as the history of French literature demonstrates, emphasis on form in the nineteenth century was to become overwhelming with the Art for Art's Sake movement, with Flaubert, and with the Symbolist poets. Even a socially committed writer like Zola was scarcely immune to the allure of form, as one can see in some of his elaborately wrought descriptive passages, like the famous 'symphony of the cheeses' in *The Belly of Paris*.

Stendhal's simplicity of style serves him well as a satirist, where his precedents clearly hark back to the eighteenth century, in particular to the Montesquieu of *Persian Letters* and the Voltaire of *L'Ingénu*. In those fictional works a neutral observer, an outsider or foreigner, presents a presumably objective depiction of the native reader's society and its institutions; stripped of their social significances, these phenomena are revealed as arbitrary codes, often masking irrational if not patently absurd positions based on little more than tradition or unexamined habit. A striking example of this technique comes in Julien's puzzled observation of the young Bishop of Agde rehearsing the gestures of a perfect apostolic benediction. The technique of the distanced observer is also employed in the presentation of the trumped-up auction, the seminary, Mme de La Mole's salon, Julien's duel and trial, and many other scenes. Again and again, a gesture is seized or arrested, then tendered for inspection in all its mechanical emptiness − and thereby the nullity of the encompassing institution or convention is revealed. The technique has entrenched itself in satire. In the twentieth century, Sartre (in *Nausea*) made good use of it in his satire of bourgeois social routines among the Sunday-morning strollers of Bouville.

And although narratorial embroidery (the interventions) abounds in *The Red and the Black*, Stendhal knew that simple directness could highlight important moments of his work by conveying them in direct discourse, without comment. This can be illustrated in the following passage (from the marginalia of *Lucien Leuwen*), where Stendhal analyses his own method of constructing dialogues:

On me. − I don't say: he enjoyed the sweet effusions of maternal tenderness, the sweet advice of a mother's heart, as in vulgar novels. I give the thing itself, the dialogue, and take care not to state *what it is* in moving phrases.

Paternity and identity

All this is to reaffirm that in Stendhal reader participation is required, that we remain the bow of the novel's sounding box. It is also to assert that beyond style lie the truly important realms of identity, those urgent questions that attended the composition of *The Life of Henry Brulard*: 'Who am I?' Julien's identity − seized as it were, beyond the end of his novel − is a long search inaugurated in the opening pages of *The Red and the Black*, where the narrator first describes how he differs physically from his brothers. The search for origins is inherent in all Oedipal narrative. In fact, the plot of Freud's

Family Romance closely matches *The Red and the Black*. Mme de Rênal the Mother is united with Julien the Son, while the Fathers (biological and adoptive) are ousted, expelled or replaced by the fables of paternity that attend Julien's maturing and rise.

Of all the themes of *The Red and the Black* (and even more so of *The Charterhouse*), paternity is the one that Stendhal most teases his reader with. After the noted dissimilarities between Julien and the other Sorels (and in the absence of any information concerning his missing mother), Julien himself exclaims that he is indeed 'a sort of orphan, hated by my father, my brothers, all my family'. He is mentored throughout by a series of father figures. The old surgeon-major, who bequeaths to Julien his library, his taste for reading, and his admiration for Napoleon, is paired (in a way that evokes the title's colour symbolism) with Abbé Chélan, who gives Julien his Latin and enough theology to point him towards an ecclesiastical career. Abbé Pirard, in whom a grateful Julien recognises authority ('I have found another father in you, sir'), offers protection in the seminary until the Marquis de La Mole completes the list of fathering, mentoring figures with whom Julien is supplied.

Abbé Pirard, the male protector who has the most affection for Julien, is constantly surprised (and often scandalised) by Julien's thoughts and conduct. It is he who admiringly wonders if his singularity might not be imputed to 'the force of blood?' By this the abbé inaugurates the suspicion that lineage might be the true explanation for Julien's otherwise inexplicable nobility of character. How ironic (from the liberal Stendhalian perspective), this implication that heredity is stronger than talent, that the best qualities are in the genes; and how in contradiction with the consistently deprecatory portrait of an anaemic, exsanguine aristocracy in the La Mole drawing room! The teasing question of Julien's paternity is brought to the fore by his rather comic duel with the Chevalier de Beauvoisis. The chevalier discovers to his horror that he has duelled with a social inferior:

'This is atrocious!' he said to his second. 'I cannot possibly admit having fought a mere secretary of M. de La Mole, and even less because my coachman stole my visiting cards.'

Fear of ridicule then leads to the planting of an honour-saving story: Julien is really the natural son of a dear friend of the Marquis de La Mole. 'This fact [sic] passed without difficulty.' Even the Marquis hears of it, saying amusedly one day to Julien, 'So now you're the natural son of a rich gentleman of the Franche-Comté, a close friend of mine!' Julien has understood perfectly well the reason for the chevalier's rumour, but the Marquis says the story suits him, and that he intends to promote its credibility.

As a further mark of his favour, the Marquis makes Julien a gift of a blue suit, and treats him as an equal when he wears it to visit him. On these occasions, Julien becomes in the Marquis's eyes the 'younger brother of the Count de Chaulnes, that is, the son of my friend the old Duke.' (This would also make Julien the Marquis's brother-in-law, and the Marquise's brother!) The Marquis continues to treat him like a son; but he also compares his attachment for 'this little abbé' to what one would feel for a pet spaniel. It is clear that the role of the man in the blue suit is to amuse the Marquis who, like all the other aristocrats of his own salon, suffers from boredom. Amusement, according to the Marquis, is 'the only real thing in life'. Finally, the Marquis ennobles Julien by authorising Abbé Pirard to reveal the 'secret' of Julien's birth. Such developments lend plausibility to Mathilde's impression at the ball that Julien looks like 'a prince in disguise'; and later she speculates on what Julien's progress would be were he suddenly recognised as the natural son of some country squire — or what his aristocratic status would be were he the son of a Spanish duke.

Stendhal is so obviously exploiting a literary tradition of origins, well entrenched in folklore (peasants bring up the king's son, who is unaware of his true origin), in comedy, and in the eighteenth-century novel, that it is legitimate to wonder if he is not doing so with some parodic intention. In this type of plot, nobility of soul is in the conclusion naturalised in a recognition scene of the protagonist's noble ancestry. The man in blue really does turn out to be the natural son of a nobleman. As Peter Brooks puts it, 'For the abbé and the Marquis, Julien's natural nobility is something of a scandal in the order of things, one that requires remotivation and authorisation through noble blood, even if illegitimately transmitted. If, like the foundling of an eighteenth-century novel or a Molière comedy, Julien were at last to find that he had been fathered by an aristocrat, this discovery would legitimate his exceptionality . . .' ('Fathers and Sons', p. 353).

Julien seems more and more absorbed into the foundling paradigm. He is eventually named 'Le chevalier Julien Sorel de La Vernaye' by the Marquis. Mathilde, in her joy, immediately obliterates his humble origins by shortening this to 'M. de La Vernaye'. And Julien himself accepts this fictional conclusion: 'After all, my novel is finished . . .' Other loose ends are tied up, notably the embarrassing presence of Père Sorel. The Marquis solves this problem by transmitting 20,000 francs to Julien as a gift from his *father* (no further precision is offered), with the suggestion that this sum be passed on to 'M. Sorel, a carpenter in Verrières, who looked after him as a child'. The Marquis attends to another vulnerable point by offering to settle his own long-standing lawsuit with Abbé de Frilair; the tacit recognition of Julien's high birth is part of the bargain. Little wonder Julien himself comes to believe the tale: 'Could it really be that I am the son of some great lord exiled in our mountains by the terrible Napoleon?' This would provide Julien with an important motivational relief: 'My hatred of my father would be proof . . . I would no longer be a monster!'

Stendhal appears about to conform to the expectations of a traditional novel ending (and indeed his own source), but as D. A. Miller notes (*Narrative and Its Discontents*, p. 210), he finally rejects closure in favour of a "suspensiveness" that evades the conventional wrapping up of dangling narrative threads. In Stendhal, fulfilment remains secondary to sustained drive and desire. Julien will never be integrated into a respectable filial paradigm, a psychological and social hierarchy that is the armature of political order. Indeed, the 'mystery' of Julien's birth is the sign of a historical contingency, an unstable legitimacy that follows in the wake of Revolutionary reversal, and which a new revolution might reassert. His reaccession to the paternal order, from which he is expelled in the opening pages of *The Red and the Black*, is blocked by his death sentence. And that sentence is the consequence of his direct challenge to the social order – the order of the Father. That rule severely punishes the revolutionary Son. This is then a double failure: not only is Julien unable to overthrow or accede to the paternal Order, he is also incapable of assuring a future for his own unborn son. That future remains problematic, not only because Mathilde is not a maternal figure, but because the mother surrogate, the loving Mother – Mme de Rênal – dies three days after Julien's execution. Julien's worst fear for his son, that he will be neglected and abandoned to the care of servants, seems a likely prospect. Thus the Oedipal cycle recommences in this adumbration of another failure to control the Son.

The question of fathers and sons in Stendhal does not only engage fables of governance and order. The illegitimate or rejected son also escapes the predestined fate explicit in paternal plans, M. de Rênal's for his sons, or the Marquis's for his daughter. The parentless child, the 'found' child, must find his own destiny and found his own order. He slips out from under the iron hand of the Father, the figure of law and authority, to live the energising existence of the *frondeur*, the *contestataire*. Mérimée said of Stendhal that everything that restricted his freedom 'was odious to him', and quoted him as saying that 'our parents and our teachers are our natural enemies when we come into the world'. Henry Brulard is the youngest revolutionary on record, and as Michel Crouzet points out (*Nature et société chez Stendhal*, p. 18), this revolt is not merely a refusal of the social order, it is first of all metaphysical. (HB's earliest memories evoked his 'horror of religion'.) And yet the figure of the Father as oppressor is a necessary component in the Son's struggle to forge his own identity. Without him, Julien's endeavour would be for nought, for in Julien's pre-Nietzschean world, as in André Gide's post-Nietzschean one, *on se pose en s'opposant*: the self is the product of resistances. An instructive counter-example can be drawn from *Lucien Leuwen*, whose eponymous hero remains incapable of finding himself, largely because of his benign, rich, and wholly indulgent father. The novel remains revealingly unfinished, and in its margins a frustrated Stendhal wondered to himself: 'But what is Lucien's character? Certainly not the energy and originality of Julien. This is impossible in the world (of 1835 and on an income of 80,000 francs).'

Patterns of love

Identity, in the end, comes primarily to the Stendhalian through love. Love is the grand theme at the centre of all Stendhal's writings, and to it he was to devote works of fiction, autobiography, and analysis. *De l'Amour* of 1822 remains a highly astute and relevant treatise on love. Its interest lies to a large extent in its directness, being (in Stendhal's own words, in the 'puff-particle' he devoted to his own work for the *Paris Monthly Review*), the *'facsimile* of all his reflections, in all their freshness and fearlessness . . .' If it presents a zeal for classification influenced by Stendhal's *Idélogue* background − for example, the four types of love, or the seven stages of the birth of love − it nevertheless admits of considerable nuance and an infinity of variations. For the reader of *The Red and the Black*, however, only two types are relevant: *l'amour-passion* and *l'amour de vanité*.

The first, as we have already seen, is passion on the grand scale, the one that carries all other considerations before it. This is Mme de Rênal's complete devotion to Julien, her placing of her love for him above social concern, above even that Christian woman's love of God. This is of course Romantic love. Yet the literary models cited in *De l'Amour* are the very ones by which Mathilde de La Mole seeks to measure her love for Julien: Dido, the Portuguese Nun, and Julien d'Etanges (heroine of *La Nouvelle Héloïse*). Mathilde also aspires to *l'amour passion*, yet Stendhal had in mind for her the character of the Parisienne who cares for her lover only so long '*as she thinks every morning that she's about to lose him*'. Here then is the bookish or cerebral love that Stendhal called *l'amour de tête*. The two heroines are often opposed, along the lines suggested by the Provincial/Parisian comparison (allomorphs of this opposition are Nature/Society, Non-reader/Reader, etc.), yet they are complementary female types as well. This much is implicit in the alternative names Stendhal imagined for his dual heroines: Mme d'Espagne and Mme de Saint-Ange. The latter name suggests the sweet, angelic nature of Mme de Rênal, the former the imperious, stormy temper of Mathilde de La Mole – what Harry Levin once called the Rebecca – Rowena motif of Stendhal's fiction (*The Gates of Horn*, p. 143). One must also give consideration to the name of Mathilde, so close to the great love of Stendhal's own life, Métilde Dembowski. (On the other hand, 'Louise', Mme de Rênal's name, is the same as Rousseau's *maman*, Louise de Warens.)

Julien's love affair with both women entails the surmounting of obstacles. In the former case, age and social rank come into play, while religious scruple is foremost in Mme de Rênal's mind. Mathilde is perhaps too preoccupied with the *idea* of love and with conforming to her literary and historical models for us to grant great depth to her emotions. While Mathilde has a rank more exalted than Mme de Rênal's to sacrifice to her lover, her contempt for social convention undercuts its value. Mme de Rênal's response is made to seem spontaneous – therefore more sincere – while Mathilde's is of a more studied variety. Julien best sums up this important distinction in the chapter title 'A Box at the Bouffes' (II, 30), suggesting the element of show that enters into her love: 'Mme de Rênal used to find reasons to obey the dictates of her heart; this young lady of high society allows her heart to be moved only when she has proved to herself with good reasons that it ought to be moved.' While Stendhal submitted the whole phenomenon of love to logical analysis in *De l'Amour*, the rational *response* to love arouses the Romantic's distrust — and so it is with Mathilde's bookishness. Mathilde projects herself and Julien into heroic historical models, appropriating the 'grandeur and audacity' of another age. The favourite roles are traced out in the family chronicles: 'the love of Marguerite de Valois for the young La Mole'. And for Mathilde, who has as great a need for obstacles as any Stendhalian creature, Julien's lack of birth becomes a desirable barrier. Mathilde also tries out the Revolutionary model, with Julien cast as Danton and herself as Mme Roland.

If we wished to place *De l'Amour* as a grid on *The Red and the Black*, we would observe both heroines progressing more or less faithfully from surprise to admiration, reaching a first crystallisation, then doubt, then a second crystallisation. Crystallisation has remained the most famous word in the Stendhalian lexicon. A leafless branch is thrown into the depths of the Salzburg salt mines, and when it is withdrawn several months later its smallest twigs are covered with brilliant salt crystals looking like diamonds: 'What I call crystallisation is the mental operation that draws from every aspect the discovery that the loved one has new perfections.' The stages of Mathilde's nascent love follow the pattern: she is astonished by his aloofness, admires his handsomeness, then crystallises for him ('I'm in love, I'm in love! It's obvious!'). She is plunged into doubt (Julien's audacity should have led him to declare his love first), then experiences a second crystallisation followed by more doubts. The superiority of the second one leaves the lover prey to these three ideas:

1 She has every perfection.
2 She loves me.
3 How can I obtain the greatest possible proof of love from her?

As Julien discovers to his great suffering, the element of doubt must be permanently sustained in the case of Mathilde's *amour de tête*. He is wounded by her confession of passing 'enthusiasms' for other young men in her father's drawing room, and in his pain he blurts out: 'So you don't love me any more, yet I adore you!' His phrase – sincere, but stupid, says the narrator – changes everything in a flash, for 'Mathilde, certain of being loved, scorned him completely.' Here Stendhal anticipates some of the most brilliant pages in *Swann in Love*, where Proust analyses the exposure of the lover who is, so to speak, dephased or out of synchronisation with the partner; for to appear to love *too much* is 'what relieves, for ever more, the loved one from loving enough'. To rekindle Mathilde's doubt is to restimulate her love for Julien, and this is the whole purpose of the Korasoff correspondence.

As we have seen, Julien in love tends to transform his triumphs into victories of class warfare. This is even more the case with Mathilde (the 'enemy') than Mme de Rênal, where he savours his preference over M. de Croisenois in a savagely satisfying review of his social inferiority: 'plebeian', 'servant', 'carpenter's son', 'poor Jura peasant'; this kind of talk also allows him to repress his scruples, and the narrator is quick to denounce these posturings and rationalisations. He and Mathilde find common ground in their reverence for models. Both take courage from the heroes of Corneille (Mathilde from his Medea, Julien from his Cid). An exterior model prods them both to play roles, roles that are no less culturally derived than the tame conventions they both despise. In fact, as F. W. J. Hemmings has remarked, these roles are for the most part incompatible, for Julien cannot be both Napoleon and Boniface de La Mole, nor can Mathilde successfully combine Josephine and Marguerite de Navarre. Not only do the roles not mesh, they cannot be successfully reenacted within the Stendhalian universe, whose vision is that of an irreversible, unrepeatable history.

Julien's models lead to some highly comical moments in his love affair with Mathilde. Her summons to climb the ladder to her room throws him into fear of a plot on his life. Is a reception party waiting in the bedroom to seize and bind him, drag him off to the cellar, shoot or poison him? or castrate him? ('Beware the fate of Abélard!') He nerves himself to the task by looking first for courage at a bust of Cardinal

Richelieu, then thinks of Julius Caesar, and reflects that he could never forgive himself for backing down. (The episode is a reprise, with comic exaggeration, of his grasping of Mme de Rênal's hand in the garden.) Julien checks his pistols, fills his pockets with daggers, and, as a last consideration, thinks: 'Besides, she's very pretty.' Role playing continues in the bedroom, as Julien recites some fine phrases from *La Nouvelle Héloïse* (a book Mathilde knows well). Mathilde, for her part, being unaccustomed to using the familiar *tu* of intimacy, listens to herself saying it. Both are extremely ill at ease, stuck at this point in what *De l'Amour* calls *l'amour de vanité*. 'Passionate love', comments the narrator, 'was still more of a model to imitate than a reality.' Mathilde finds it her duty to reward her courageous lover. Anticipating Madame Bovary, she does not experience in this night the complete bliss that novels speak of, and Julien feels only the satisfactions of *amour propre*.

When Julien has won the Korasoff battle against Mathilde, his deep instincts take him back to Mme de Rênal; rereading the *Mémorial de Sainte-Hélène*, his head and his heart 'were working unknown to him. This heart is very different from Mme de Rênal's', he tells himself, 'but he did not go further.' Presumably, had he continued the comparison between the two women it would have favoured Mme de Rênal. In his projected review, Stendhal specifically termed Mathilde's love *amour de tête*, and Mme de Rênal's *amour de cœur* — a synonym of love-passion. (One cannot avoid making the connection, a rather Romantically grotesque one, between *amour de tête* and the final scene in which Mathilde carries Julien's severed head on her lap; nor can one forget Stendhal's admiration for a Salome painting in the Uffizi.) And when Mme de Rênal tells Julien she loves him more than God, we have touched the ultimate gauge of Romantic passion. Julien's conquests bring pleasure without happiness.

The last chapter of *De l'Amour* opposed Don Juan to Werther and Saint-Preux (again, *La Nouvelle Héloïse*). While the Spanish seducer is fortunate in the eyes of the world, his triumphs are the result of conscious, or, rather, self-conscious, seductions. Yet self-conscious strategies are irreconcilable with *imprévu* and a host of Stendhalian qualities: 'Instead of losing himself in the enchanting reveries of crystallisation, [Don Juan] thinks like a general about the success of his manoeuvres, and in a word kills love instead of enjoying it more than other men, as the herd believes.' Werther's (or Saint-Preux's) happiness is not modelled on reality, but on his desires; in short, it is founded on the imagination. Don Juan's role is brilliant and public, but Werther's is sweet and private, and finally more intensely felt. While this is not an apologia for Platonic love, Werther's superiority is clearly of a spiritual sort that reserves large areas for flights of the chimaerical imagination:

The pleasure that one meets with a pretty woman desired for two weeks and kept for three months, is *different* from the pleasure one finds with a mistress desired for three years and kept for ten.

The mistress desired for three years is still met with trembling; and, he would say to Don Juan, the man who trembles is not blasé: 'The pleasures of love are always in proportion to fear.' Werther, then, is happier, and with this praise of tenderness in love, the reader is returned to the idyll of Vergy, and to the Rousseauist patterns that Stendhal finally favours in love. What finally raises Mme de Rênal above Mathilde is not the Oedipal satisfactions of maternal love she affords, but rather her aptitude for solitude and privacy. She and Julien are deeply joined in this predilection, strongly hinted at in an early chapter title borrowed from Goethe, 'Elective affinities'. Thus Mathilde's grand strivings in order to save Julien from conviction and execution go against the grain of his deepest inclination; as the narrator writes, her interventions betray 'a secret need to astonish the public by the extent of her love and the sublimity of her undertakings' (II, 39).

The shooting

If Julien comes to a last-minute understanding of all these peculiarly Stendhalian truths, it is thanks to the most scandalous act of the entire novel: his attempted murder of Mme de Rênal. Generations of readers and commentators have denounced or rationalised the shooting. What constitutes the problem are the abruptness of the act and the ellipsis of motivation, for in the space of one page Julien reads Mme de Rênal's letter, bids Mathilde adieu, and travels to Verrières to fire upon his former mistress.

Emile Faguet, a conservative critic at the turn of the century, was the first commentator to complain that Julien's actions (and those of cooler-headed characters around him) were implausible. The ending was 'quite bizarre and, in truth, a bit more false than is permissible'. How could a character so scheming as Julien Sorel plausibly undertake – so precipitously – such a calamitous step? Dealing with this objection, and declining to respond in psychological terms, a number of *Stendhaliens* (Léon Blum, Jean Prévost, Maurice Bardèche) pointed to Stendhal's source: Berthet fired and Stendhal obligingly followed his prototype to its dramatic conclusion. This 'source explanation' is intended to be compelling because of its reliance on life (a real-life attempted murder), as opposed to the arbitrariness of a cultural construct (a fictional attempted murder), but it is tautological, for it merely justifies one text in terms of another, anterior text – the phenomenon called 'overdetermination'. Yet it adumbrates a more modern, textually oriented view, wherein the crime figures as *The Red and the Black*'s own recognition (and consequent rejection) of the smug plot of the traditional nineteenth-century *arriviste* novel. That self-recognition is explicit in Julien's phrase, 'My novel is finished.' In these terms, the shooting would be an attempt to unwrite the plot in the conventional pattern and to restart novelistic paths: whom will Mathilde now marry? what will become of Julien's son? And not least, what will now be thought of Julien? The novel would then reach towards a redefinition of the self outside the constricting definitions of plot; it would successfully resist closure.

Many readers find comfort in the traditional psychological argumentations, of which the classical interpretation is that of Henri Martineau, who argued that Julien was perfectly capable of committing a *crime passionnel*, and expended considerable energy in mounting a clinical explanation of the hypnotic state Julien finds himself in: 'the silence of lucid hypnosis'. F. W. J. Hemmings saw Julien as acting with 'absolute logic'. He chooses to do what would be least expected of an ambitious schemer in order to save his sense of honour and to efface Mme de Rênal's slur: 'It is an act of self-justification.' P.-G. Castex also argued for full lucidity, and saw Julien as fulfilling Stendhal's vision of the lower class's brute energy faced by an entrenched but exhausted aristocracy. According to Gérard Genette, Julien's crime is left unexplained so that it may exploit 'the wild individuality that characterises the unforeseeability of great actions' ('Stendhal', p. 77).

Certainly there are elements of truth and degrees of convincingness in all these interpretations. Julien's somnambulism is a state we have previously encountered him in, as Charles du Bos was the first to point out. After his grand political discussion with Altamira, and a night spent reading the history of the Revolution, Julien is virtually unconscious of Mathilde's presence in the library the following morning – until the sharp noise of breaking glass 'awakens him at last'. This would prepare the reader for the moment when Julien 'comes to' after the shooting. Travel in this state would be accomplished swiftly, and there is a precedent for this, too. Julien rushes from Strasbourg to Paris with 'a nearly incredible rapidity', and, similarly, he makes the trip back to Verrières (roughly the same distance) by an equally 'rapid way', arriving in an obvious state of shock. The abruptness of Julien's departure for Verrières to kill Mme de Rênal is prepared by his action in Paris. When Mathilde outrages him by lamenting that she gave herself 'to the first comer', his spontaneous reaction was to seize an antique sword and run her through with it. (Thus it is Mme de Rênal who will experience the Romantic thrill of 'having been nearly killed' by her lover; ' "To die by Julien's hand", she says, would be the greatest of joys.') He can barely make the gunsmith understand his request for a pair of pistols, nor is he in a state to load them himself. His first shot misses, yet he is standing only 'a few steps' behind Mme de Rênal, and his second shot fails to kill her. This is the performance of a man who practised firearms daily in Paris with a famous instructor. Even after Julien makes a partial return to full consciousness, he is knocked to the ground by a fleeing woman and manhandled into gaol by a single policeman: 'all this was carried out very quickly, and he was unconscious of it'.

Julien shoots to avenge himself, as he writes Mathilde; as he tells himself, 'I was atrociously offended.' His impetuous act surprises only those readers — there have been many of them — who neglect his prickly sense of honour, his gift for *imprévu*, and see in him mainly a scheming hypocrite of precisely the sort that Mme de Rênal describes in her fatal letter. For Julien, its most stinging misrepresentations are the allegations of cupidity and fortune hunting — and of being a seducer. Now Julien has always expressed his scorn for those who think only of money, like Lieutenant Robert of 'A-Imagination' — but as he well knows, to outsiders he is particularly vulnerable to versions of these accusations. For he is poor yet ambitious, and has indeed 'seduced' two women more from pride and ambition than from passion. In neither case does he fall in love until after the seduction.

It is difficult to believe that Julien acts with perfect logic, however, for in the heat of the moment we have previously seen him take arms when he thinks he has been wronged: he fires his pistols at the lackeys who beset him in the courtyard of the Hôtel de Beauvoisis, and there is the incident with Mathilde and the sword. And only after learning that Mme de Rênal is not dead does Julien really emerge from his catatonic state: 'only in that instant ended the state of physical irritation and half-madness he had been plunged into since his departure from Paris for Verrières' (II, 36). Moreover, Julien tells himself in prison that he sought to kill Mme de Rênal out of ambition or for love of Mathilde, so it will not do to close our eyes to the baser aspects of his motives. Julien, for his part, never flinches from recognising this: 'Ah! I loved Mme de Rênal, but my behaviour was atrocious. There, as elsewhere, I abandoned simple, modest worth for what was flashy' (II, 42).

The best we can say is that Julien's crime saves him from his ambitious self and returns him to his better one. Echoing Goethe, Julien reflects that it is true that man bears two natures within himself — two radically different selves. Finally, we cannot fail to note that in his famous self-review, Stendhal merely summarises the facts of the shooting, without seeking to explain them. His comment regarding the extravagant actions of his characters was simply to assert that 'These follies are astonishing, without ceasing to be natural. There lies the merit of M. de Stendhal.' Julien's apparent lack of motivation, all the elided, empty space where motives may be supposed to dwell, must stand as the shadow of an unknown, that is, a terrain veiled by censorship and desire, as a prefiguration of the Freudian unconscious. It is ironic that Stendhal, the rationalist *Idéologue*, should have sensed this realm.

Chapter 3

Stendhal's mirrors

'the purpose of playing, whose end, both at the first and now, was and is, to hold, as 'twere, the mirror up to nature'.*Hamlet*, III, 2

Stendhal's commitment to truth before style and his serio-satirical designation of the novel as a mirror of society have ensured *The Red and the Black* a leading place in the history of literary realism. Yet Stendhal enjoyed scant popularity during his own time, and was known less for his novels than for his writings on travel and music. He was more socially than intellectually known, enjoying the reputation of a *salonnard* whose caustic wit gave rise to the waggish phrase, '*Stendhal, c'est un scandale.*' This presumably gives us a clue to the nineteenth-century pronunciation of his name. The small audiences his novels addressed are figured in the famous *envoi* (in English) of *The Red and the Black*: 'To the Happy Few.'

We have seen that HB of *The Life of Henry Brulard* entertained serious doubts concerning the durability and probability of literary fame. Certainly nothing in reader reaction to *The Red and the Black* could have encouraged him to think otherwise. Early criticism of the novel was harsh, centring on the double accusation of the immorality and the implausibility of the characters. Julien's conduct appeared contradictory (even to Stendhal's friend Mérimée), and the conservative critic Jules Janin denounced Mathilde as 'crazy'. Yet Stendhal has always had his admirers, too, and the first and most famous of them remains Balzac, whose enthusiasm for *The Charterhouse of Parma* was both generous and misguided.

The first wave of Stendhalian enthusiasts arose in the university in the 1850s. This was the generation of Hippolyte

Taine and Francisque Sarcey, whose master at the Ecole Normale Supérieure, Jacquinet, was a partisan of Stendhal, whom he viewed as a rampart against Romantic sentimentalism and as the heir of a sceptical, Voltairean tradition. Stendhal, for these men and women, practised a positivistic science of the human heart; he was a clear-headed analyst, and at a time when his great autobiographical texts were still unpublished, his latent Romantic streak passed unnoticed. Indeed, it is not ironic that during his lifetime Stendhal should have been considered as a defender of Romanticism, and after his death as its detractor.

Sainte-Beuve had never felt comfortable with Stendhal's works; in 1857, reacting against Taine's praise for him as the 'greatest psychologist of the century', he declared that for his part he had recently reread Stendhal's novels ('always botched') and found them 'detestable'.

This was too severe for Zola, even though he did not hold entirely favourable views of Stendhal. While including him among the precursors of Naturalism (but as a link with the eighteenth-century novel), Zola also complained that Julien's behaviour was as full of adventurous surprises as D'Artagnan's. He deplored the absence of milieu in *The Red and the Black* ('he cares neither for the house where his hero grew up, nor the horizons where he lived'), and turning Stendhal's mirror image against him, wrote that Stendhal's looking glass yielded only truncated portraits: 'this mirror reflects only the head of man, the noble part, without presenting the body or the surrounding places' (*The Naturalist Novelists*, p. 96). For Henry James, Stendhal was simply immoral.

The cult of Stendhal became particularly intense with the publication of his autobiographical writings in the 1880s − a time that he himself had predicted for his literary resurrection. (Ignorance of these writings had not prevented Andrew Paton, an Edinburgh native, from producing the first full-length biography of Stendhal in 1874.) The novelist Paul Bourget could remember conversations between established writers vying to prove their superior knowledge of *The Red and the Black*: 'One would say, *M. de La Vernaye would be at your feet* . . . and the other would continue, *overcome with gratitude* . . . The game was to find one's colleague in flagrant ignorance of a single one of the adjectives in the book' (*Essays in Contemporary Psychology*, p. 310). Yet reviewing a new edition of *The Red and the Black*, Bourget also thought that the paradox of Stendhal's works was that they were both famous and uninfluential: 'Neither in the novels of Flaubert, nor in those of the Goncourt brothers, nor in the studies of M. Zola himself or of M. Daudet, nor in those of M. de Maupassant and M. Huysmans, can one discover a feature that suggests, even slightly, the very special and very recognisable "hand" of the author of *The Red and the Black*' (*Studies and Portraits*, I, p. 261).

By this time a knowledge and taste for Russian literature, thanks to Viscount de Vogüé's efforts, was penetrating into France. But the changed literary horizon did not deter the establishment critic Emile Faguet from expressing bewilderment at Julien's actions, and dismissing Stendhal as a bad stylist who observed the lower and middle classes as a kind of 'Saint-Simon of the table d'hôte'.

Around 1908–10, Stendhal was admired by the young writers of the *Nouvelle Revue Française* group: André Suarès, Charles Du Bos, Léon Blum, Ramon Fernandez, and of course André Gide. Gide, whose opinion remained rather equivocal, praised Stendhal's fierce individualism and elusiveness, but would have sacrificed everything else for *The Life of Henry Brulard* (preface to *Armance*, p. ii).

Nor were Stendhal's admirers exclusively French. Gabriele D'Annunzio was a member of the committee formed to raise a memorial to him. Nietzsche had saluted him as a 'strange Epicurean and man of interrogation, the last great psychologist of France' (*Beyond Good and Evil*, no. 254), and Joseph Conrad, denouncing 'the fettering dogmas of some romantic, realistic, or naturalistic creed in the free work of the imagination', refuted those (meaning Zola) who would claim Stendhal as a prophet of Naturalism, and praised Stendhal's liberty of imagination: 'Stendhal himself would have accepted no limitations of his freedom . . . He wrote his two great novels, which so few people have read, in a spirit of fearless liberty' (*Notes on Life and Letters*, pp. 9–10).

Paul Valéry found Stendhal's *tone* the most strikingly individual in all literature. That tone was marked by liveliness, with 'allusions which can be even obscure, abrupt transitions, leaps, parentheses; the conversational tone and the avoidance of affectation'. Yet Valéry had strong doubts about any writer's ability to achieve truth, particularly in autobiographical writings (*Variety II*, p. 112).

It was in the *entre-deux-guerres* period that Stendhal began to attract the attention of first-rate scholars and critics like Albert Thibaudet, Jean Prévost and, above all, Henri Martineau, who indefatigably chronicled every detail of Stendhal's life, wrote critical and biographical studies, and published what remained for a long time the only complete edition of Stendhal's works, the famous small format Divan edition (1927–37) in 79 volumes. Victor Del Litto carried on in the tradition of Martineau, occupying a chair reserved for a Stendhal scholar at the University of Grenoble (today occupied by Philippe Berthier).

A landmark event in the history of Stendhal studies and of literary realism in general certainly came about with the publication in 1946 of Erich Auerbach's influential study, *Mimesis*. Zola had already stated that *The Red and the Black* would be incomprehensible if one did not take into account the period in which it was conceived (*The Naturalist Novelists*, p. 93). Auerbach hailed *The Red and the Black* as a work in which 'contemporary political and social conditions are woven into the action in a manner more detailed and more real than had been exhibited in any earlier novel, and indeed in any works of literary art except those expressly purporting to be politico-satirical tracts' (chapter 18, 'In the Hôtel de La Mole'). Auerbach's chapter on *The Red and the Black* had begun with his quoting of the scene where Julien complains to Abbé Pirard of the boredom he experiences at the La Mole table; of it, Auerbach wrote that it would be 'almost incomprehensible without a most accurate and detailed knowledge of the political situation, the social stratification, and the economic circumstances of a perfectly definite historical moment . . .' *Race, moment, milieu*: if these echoes of Taine's positivism obviously shape his judgement, Auerbach's meaning is nonetheless unambiguous: the modern consciousness of reality, historically informed, 'began to find literary form for the first time in Henri Beyle of Grenoble'. Stendhal was alert to historical change and relativism, constantly wondering what the nature of his readers would be in 1880 or 1930. Auerbach called this frame of mind Stendhal's 'time perspective'. Stendhal is the founder of a modern realism that represents man as 'embedded in a total reality, political, social, and economic, which is concrete and constantly evolving . . .'

While stating that Julien is much more of a hero than the characters of the later realists such as Balzac, to say nothing of Flaubert, Auerbach pointed out that the heroes of pre-Romantic novels 'betray a sometimes morbid aversion to entering into contemporary life'. (Auerbach could have added that Stendhal was also the creator of the 'unheroic hero'.) Yet in Stendhal, the reader confronts 'the resistance of the real and the historical'. (Auerbach seemed wholly impervious to the Romantic dimension of Stendhal's realism.)

The influence of Saussurean structural linguistics on literary studies since the 1960s was to transform our views of the very nature of the literary work of art. Whereas Auerbach unproblematically asserted the 'entanglement' of *The Red and the Black* with the real and the historical, modern critical developments, viewing the text as a closed, auto-referential structure, would relegate the historical component of Stendhal's novel to the status of an *hors-texte*: a body of considerations external and irrelevant to the self-regulating nature of verbal art. Thus 'realism' in some theoreticians' minds became itself relativised or historicised as a false problem of literary history. Moreover, before the Structuralist emphasis on language in its own right (*langue vs. parole*), scant attention was actually paid to the medium of apprehension itself – the mirror of reality. Much was made of Stendhal's style (chiefly in comments on its sparseness), yet little thought had been expended on a presumably transparent window on the world. Champfleury, an early champion of Courbet's realism in art and author of a collection of critical essays entitled *Le Réalisme*, proclaimed that writing was as simple as speaking: 'What I see enters my head, flows down into my pen, and becomes what I saw' (preface to his *Domestic Tales*, 1852). Champfleury never paused to consider that his mirror was made of ink.

If the thrust of realism — to be 'true to life' — is undermined by the philosophy of language that posits all relationships between words and things as arbitrary, fiction can nevertheless lay powerful claims to being a mode of cognition. Indeed, its function as a primer of post-Revolutionary social relations and ethics was one obvious factor in the continuing rise of the novel's popularity in the nineteenth century.

It is impossible to deny the nineteenth-century impact of realism and of *The Red and the Black* on the development of the novel. Although it was Balzac who was the first to use the key term *milieu* in its full sociological import, it is hard to grant to the *Human Comedy*, despite its all-encompassing pretensions to depict the whole of the society of its time, the specific gravity and grittiness that unadulterated realism demands. Despite Auerbach's view that Balzac and Stendhal were co-creators of modern realism, and despite Zola's opinion that Balzac was the 'father of our naturalist novel', it is difficult not to grant precedence, if not absolute pride of place, to Stendhal.

The nineteenth-century French novel tradition, with Flaubert and the Naturalists, continued to build on the realistic foundation laid down by Stendhal and Balzac. Proust explicitly claimed Balzac as his model for the depiction of society. The leading French novelists from the 1930s through the 1950s — Malraux, Mauriac, Sartre, and Camus — clearly swim in the mainstream whose source reaches back to the mirror novel of 1830.

In the 1960s, the *nouveau roman* set out to disrupt the comfortable conventions of the traditional novel — the confident connection between text and world, symbol and object. Its intention, according to Alain Robbe-Grillet (the novelist with whom the New Novel was most closely associated), was to restore independence to the world of things, to free it from the symbolising, humanising intent of the author (*For a New Novel*, pp. 20–1). Objects in the New Novel would no longer be an extension or repository of abstract, mental projects — rather they would become mere optical resistances. Walls, presumably, would signify only themselves, and would no longer, like those of Verrières, 'stand for' the class divisions of a certain epoch. By practising a rigorous objectivity, a veritable *chosisme*, the New Novel's surface geometries would achieve an autonomy of being, an empirical status putting Stendhal's poor mirror realism to shame. This goal, it will surprise no-one to learn, was far from being reached in Robbe-Grillet; exegetes were quick to demonstrate the symbolic value of this or that object or sequence in his novels.

The New New Novel, or *Tel Quel* novel (so named after the avant-garde journal), of which Philippe Sollers is the supreme practitioner, is an attempt to remedy these shortcomings. Barthes, with respect to Sollers, confidently wrote of 'sending representation on holiday' (*Sollers the Writer*, p. 53). *Nombres* (1968) is such a novel; it allegedly succeeds, according to Jean Ricardou, not merely in subverting the category of the character, but in abolishing it; it foregrounds its narrative means and does not simply turn the process of representation against itself; rather, through the play of intertextuality, it *annuls* representation: 'The novel is no longer a mirror that is walked along a road; it is the mirror effect everywhere acting on its own' (*For a Theory of the New Novel*, p. 262). Thus, far from claiming entanglement with concrete reality, the contemporary work asserts and privileges its autonomy as verbal art, glorying in the free play of the Word and promoting the 'free-floating signifier'. And we must also allude, however briefly, to the contemporary Latin American novel, with its playful violations of mimesis ('magic realism') and its awareness of its own fictional status ('metafiction').

While novelists seek to annul mimesis and promote *écriture* (permanent deferral of easy explication and absorption), others, like Foucault, or Deleuze and Guattari, have preferred ideological charges against it. The *vraisemblance* sought by the mimetic text makes it, in their view, the accomplice of authoritarianism. As Christopher Prendergast has written in *The Order of Mimesis* (pp. 52–7), it presents a world or order of things-as-they-are, which by virtue of its familiarity is closed to criticism. But the taken-for-grantedness of this descriptive world often masks a prescriptive and normative discourse – another way of saying that the cultural is trying to fob itself off as the natural. So mimesis is implicated in a discourse of power, of the propagation and reinforcement of the *doxa* (the opposite of truth) of general opinion, that body of mystifications of bourgeois culture that Barthes demystified in *Mythologies*. For Barthes, mimetic discourse was uncritical repetition and conformism. Mimesis is thus a function and characteristic of the text of closure, which he termed *lisible* ('readable'). Barthes vaunted the liberating openness of the *scriptible* ('writable') – like Sollers's *Nombres* – that resists the normative, ordering operations of the *lisible*. I have already suggested several ways in which *The Red and the Black*, the mirror text, paradoxically eludes closure, *lisibilité*, and even mimesis. Moreover, it must be noted that had Stendhal been consciously cultivating the kind of art we call realistic today, he would have been unlikely to pass to the writing of *La Chartreuse de Parme* – a work conceived in an entirely different mode. Stendhal, with his *espagnolisme*, was just as strongly attracted to the sublime as to mimesis.

Realism characteristically accumulates details – 'quiddities' – to produce the impression of reality. But can the twentieth-century reader connect with a collocation of nineteenth-century specificities? Convincing fictional realism should also operate at some abstract level in order to tap the general and the common, even the universal dimension of human experience, without which the mimetic text would die of its topicality. It must glide between the individual and the typical.

With its subtitle and epigraph, *The Red and the Black*

aggressively advances and prefigures its most famous claim: to be the replication of a certain society. That Stendhal attempted to render a faithful portrait of his age is undeniable; he never doubted that this end could be achieved through fictional means. Stendhal's chronicle novel, however, is not the transcription of archival researches, the writing up of a story already contained in a mass of available historical data. Nineteenth-century historiography, whose theoretical premises were being conceptualised about the same time that the realistic novel was evolving its own claims to truth, would have posited a radical difference between its own scientific aims and methods and the imaginative ones of the novel — a genre of writing devoted to an invented reality. On one hand, history; on the other, story. Yet as the French word *histoire* neatly demonstrates, there is so much overlap between the activities as to render the distinction dubious. Hayden White has remarked that the nineteenth-century historian envisaged his task as a willingness to go to the archives without preconceptions, then write the story found there. 'The notion that the historian himself emplotted the events found in the documents was only vaguely glimpsed . . .' (*Metahistory*, p. 142). Thus the historian's text was not merely the unproblematic transcription (the mirror) of a documentary reality, but the result of unconscious 'poetic' (i.e. literary) choices themselves connected with philosophical and ideological positions: 'accuracy in the details was often confused with the truth of the meaning of the story'.

Literary mimesis blurs the demarcations between fiction and history. Which is which? Already in 1864, the Goncourts had written in their *Journal* that the novel of their day had little to do with the times of Balzac. The modern novel was composed with *documents*, just like history: 'Historians are tellers [*raconteurs*] of the past; novelists, tellers of the present' (*Journal*, VII, 15). Thus the boundary between two essentially narrative activities becomes indistinct, diffuse. Historians can become novelists unaware, and vice-versa.

Appropriately enough, this fluidity is staged in *The Red and the Black* in one of those specular moments of textual self-awareness to which André Gide gave the name of *mise en abyme*. This is a scene that foregrounds the story-telling act itself. In prison, Julien invites two prisoners into his cell to share a bottle of champagne. One of them offers to recount his life, but for a price:

> 'If you give me twenty francs', said one of them to Julien, 'I'll tell you my life in detail. It's *first-rate.*'
> 'But will you tell me lies?'
> 'Not at all', he replied; 'my friend there is jealous of my twenty francs; he'll tell on me if I lie.'

The scene enacts the precariousness, the fragility of the realist novel's claim to truth that inheres in the impossibility of separating fact from fiction — particularly where truth might confusingly be 'stranger than fiction'. An important shift in perspective helps dramatise the problem: from author/actor of his own novel, Julien is changed into a paying member of the audience. Now his first fear is to be told a *tale*. Although the witness (History in the guise of the friend) is present to rectify or authenticate the story, the audience's fear of falling victim to a confidence trick cannot be assuaged. For the English speaker, the ambiguity of the expression 'to tell a tale/a story' nicely approximates the double meaning of *histoire*. And *The Red and the Black* is certainly a book that avails itself of and exploits the overlapping narrative categories of history/story, reality/fiction, and indeed, truth/tale. Where, finally, is the 'truth' of the Battle of Waterloo, in the narrations of history or the story of Fabrice Del Dongo? Where the 'truth' of the 1848 Revolution, in Ernest Lavisse's *History of France* or Flaubert's *Sentimental Education*? So realism, at the level of emplotment, where narrative categories are interwoven, suffuses the facts with the sense of a lived experience.

Guide to further reading

English readers are well served by fairly recent biographies of Stendhal: those of Joanna Richardson (London, 1974), Gita May (New York, 1977), and Robert Alter (New York, 1979) can all be recommended. *The Red and the Black* has proved to be quite a challenge to its English translators; two of the best are by C. K. Scott Moncrieff (London, 1926) and Robert M. Adams (New York, 1969). Scott Moncrieff's reputation as a translator of French masterpieces (notably Proust's *Remembrance of Things Past*) is high, but his version of *The Red and the Black* is formal and even stiff. Adams's is more colloquial; his edition includes an informative section on backgrounds and sources, and excerpts from critical studies of the novel. The translations of Margaret Shaw (Harmondsworth, 1953, as *Scarlet and Black*) and of Lloyd Parks (New York, 1970) may also be recommended.

The Restoration is sympathetically treated in G. de Bertier de Sauvigny's exhaustive *La Restauration* (Paris, 1955) and more briefly in Alfred Cobban's *A History of Modern France*, vol. 2 (Harmondsworth, 1961).

In English, the best general studies of Stendhal's novels are Victor Brombert, *Stendhal: Fiction and the Themes of Freedom* (New York, 1968), and F. W. J. Hemmings, *Stendhal: A Study of His Novels* (Oxford, 1964). Gilbert Chaitin, *The Unhappy Few: A Psychological Study of the Novels of Stendhal* (Bloomington, 1972), takes a Freudian approach to Stendhal, as does (augmented by a feminist perspective) Carol A. Mossman, *The Narrative Matrix. Stendhal's 'Le Rouge et le Noir'* (Lexington, 1984). Robert M. Adams, *Stendhal: Notes on a Novelist* (New York, 1959) is more personal and biographical, with excellent pages on Stendhal and Destutt de Tracy. Marcel Gutwirth's *Stendhal* (New York, 1971) is an elegantly written introduction to our author, as is Michael Wood's *Stendhal* (London, 1971).

Emile Talbot, *Stendhal and Romantic Esthetics* (Lexington, 1985) situates Stendhal in the artistic debates of his times (the *beau idéal*, for instance), while Margaret Tillett, *Stendhal: The Background to the Novels* (Oxford, 1971), emphasises Stendhal's non-fictional writings.

Rewarding chapters on Stendhal in books with broader coverage or interests can be found in Harry Levin, *The Gates of Horn* (New York and Oxford, 1963), René Girard, *Deceit, Desire, and the Novel* (translation by Y. Freccero, Baltimore, 1965), Leo Bersani, *From Balzac to Beckett* (New York, 1970), Elizabeth Tenenbaum, *The Problematic Self* (Cambridge, Mass., 1977), and D. A. Miller, *Narrative and Its Discontents* (Princeton, 1981; on Stendhal and closure). Originally a *PMLA* article, Peter Brooks's 'The Novel and the Guillotine, or Fathers and Sons in *Le Rouge et le Noir*' is reprinted in his *Reading for the Plot. Design and Intention in Narrative* (New York, 1984).

An introductory study in fewer than 70 pages is *Stendhal: Le Rouge et le Noir* (London, 1973), by John Mitchell. Interpretations of the title have been summarised in an article by Patrick Pollard: 'Colour Symbolism in *Le Rouge et le Noir*' (*Modern Language Review*, 1981), and an entire monograph has been devoted to the title: Serge Bokobza, *Contribution à la titrologie romanesque: variations sur le titre 'Le Rouge et le Noir*' (Geneva, 1986).

In French, the various Pléiade editions of Stendhal's novels, autobiographical writings, and correspondence by Henri Martineau and Victor Del Litto are filled with informative introductions and notes. Martineau's *L'Oeuvre de Stendhal* (Paris, 1945) collects the prefaces to the Divan edition. The same author's *Petit dictionnaire stendhalien* (Paris, 1948) gives biographical information on figures of Stendhal's times. These are well worth consulting. Del Litto's *La Vie intellectuelle de Stendhal* (Paris, 1959) is an exhaustive examination of his intellectual formation; Del Litto is also the author of the standard *Vie de Stendhal* (Paris, 1965).

George Blin's *Stendhal et les problèmes du roman* (Paris, 1954) is an admired study of novelistic technique; Victor Brombert's *Stendhal et la voie oblique* (New Haven, 1954) concentrates on the narrator in Stendhal. The titles of Grahame Jones, *L'Ironie de Stendhal* (Lausanne, 1966) and Francine Marill Albérès, *Le Naturel chez Stendhal* (Paris 1956) are self-explanatory. Jean Prévost's much admired *La Création chez Stendhal* (Paris, 1951; original edn Lyon, 1942) is a general study of all of Stendhal's works, as is Maurice Bardèche's *Stendhal romancier* (Paris, 1947). Shoshana Felman, *La 'Folie' dans l'oeuvre romanesque de Stendhal* (Paris, 1971), takes a structuralist approach to a key term in *The Red and the Black*; semiotics is served in Madeleine Simon's *Sémiotisme de Stendhal* (Geneva, 1980).

Simone de Beauvoir briefly praised the authenticity of Stendhal's female characters in *Le Deuxième Sexe* (Paris, 1949); *The Second Sex* (translation by H. M. Parshley, New York, 1953). Jean-Pierre Richard's 'Connaissance et tendresse chez Stendhal' (*Littérature et sensation*, Paris, 1954) was a corrective to the rationalist view of Stendhal prevalent in earlier criticism; the first part has been published as 'Knowledge and Tenderness in Stendhal' (translation by Paul A. Archambault) in Victor Brombert (ed.), *Stendhal. A Collection of Critical Essays* (Englewood Cliffs, 1962). Jean Starobinski's great essay on the uses of the mask, 'Stendhal pseudonyme', was published in his *L'Oeil vivant* (Paris, 1961); a portion appears as 'Truth in Masquerade' (translation by B. A. B. Archer), in the previous entry. Gérard Genette's 'Stendhal' (*Figures II*, Paris, 1969; translation by Alan Sheridan in Genette, *Figures of Literary Discourse*, New York, 1982) deals with the complex interrelationships of the whole body of Stendhal's writings.

Michel Crouzet, prolific and prolix, has devoted a number of lengthy studies to Stendhal, of which *Stendhal et le langage* (Paris, 1981) deals with crucial problems of self, society, and speech in a nineteenth-century historical context. His *Stendhal et l'Italianité* (Paris, 1982) deals with a crucial question, and his *Nature et société chez Stendhal* (Paris, 1985) complements Albérès on *le naturel*. Philippe Berthier's *Stendhal et la sainte famille* (Paris, 1983) traces the fictional reenactment of HB's family drama; the Family Romance as it applies to *The Red and the Black* has been studied in Marthe Robert's *Roman des origines et origines du roman* (Paris, 1972). Béatrice Didier's *Stendhal autobiographe* (Paris, 1983) is authoritative on its subject. Roland Barthes's last article, 'On échoue toujours à parler de ce qu'on aime' (*Tel Quel*, 1980), dealt with Stendhal's passion for his '*matrie*', Italy.

Brief introductions to *The Red and the Black* include P.-G Castex's '*Le Rouge et le Noir' de Stendhal* (Paris, 1970), which approaches the novel from the perspective of literary history; Geneviève Mouillaud's book of the same title (Paris, 1973) is largely, but not exclusively, a Freudian reading; Christine Klein and Paul Lidsky's '*Le Rouge et le Noir'. Stendhal* Paris, 1971 is an eighty-page primer.

Since 1958, Stendhalians possess their own specialised journal: *Stendhal Club*. Del Litto is its editor. In addition to the articles, there is a section on Stendhalian happenings of note (*Chronique*), and a yearly bibliography.

This listing omits, with deep apologies, a number of fine, but unfortunately untranslated, Italian contributions to Stendhal studies by Benedetto, Cordié, Simone, Trompeo, etc. However, G. Tomasi di Lampedusa's 'Notes on Stendhal: *The Red and the Black*' appears in Adams's edition (see above). For understandable reasons, the tradition of Stendhal studies in Italy is a very strong one.

Mimesis, as indicated, goes back to *The Republic*. Its modern applications, as regards the novel, are to be found in Auerbach's *Mimesis* (translation by Willard Trask, Princeton, 1953). Auerbach's chapter, entitled 'In the Hôtel de La Mole', discussed in chapter 3, should be supplemented by his 'Epilegomena zu *Mimesis*' (*Romanische Forschungen*, 1954). Georg Lukács's 'Balzac and Stendhal' (*Studies in European Realism*, London, 1950) brings a Marxist perspective to bear on the emergence of realism. J. P. Stern's *On Realism* (London, 1973) contributes the useful term of 'the middle distance' to indicate that the artistic perspective of realism is suspended between the extremes of a microscopic presentation of objects and the broad 'skeleton structures of the world' (p. 55). Christopher Prendergast's stimulating book, *The Order of Mimesis* (Cambridge, 1986), examines the phenomenon in the context of contemporary critical theory, and devotes a chapter to the question of verisimilitude in *The Red and the Black*. The subject had earlier received treatment in Gérard Genette's 'Vraisemblance et motivation' (*Figures III*, Paris, 1969). See also 'Convention and Naturalisation' in Jonathan Culler's *Structuralist Poetics* (London, 1975). A contemporary philosopher's treatment of mimesis can be found in Richard Rorty's *Philosophy and the Mirror of Nature* (Princeton, 1979). Although it is concerned with nineteenth-century historiography rather than realist fiction, Hayden White's *Metahistory* (Baltimore, 1973) has much to teach us about the art of narration in historical writing.

Finally, for an overview of realism's repercussions in other European literatures (*verismo, costumbrismo*, the Russians, etc.), see F. W. J. Hemmings (editor), *The Age of Realism* (Harmondsworth, 1974).